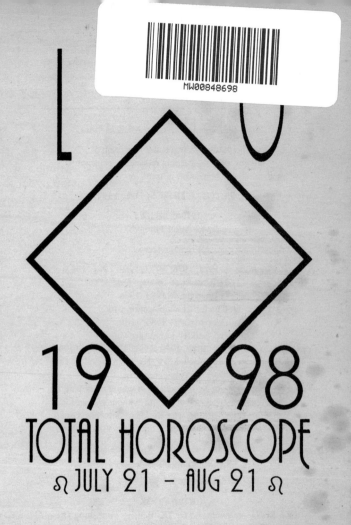

1998
TOTAL HOROSCOPE
♌ JULY 21 – AUG 21 ♌

JOVE BOOKS, NEW YORK

Astrological perspectives by Michael Lutin

The publishers regret that they cannot
answer individual letters requesting personal
horoscope information.

1998 TOTAL HOROSCOPE: LEO

PRINTING HISTORY
Jove edition/July 1997

All rights reserved.

Copyright © 1977, 1978, 1979, 1980, 1981, 1982
by Grosset & Dunlap, Inc.
Copyright © 1983, 1984
by Charter Communications, Inc.
Copyright © 1985, 1986
by The Berkley Publishing Group.
Copyright © 1987, 1988, 1989, 1990, 1991, 1992, 1993, 1994, 1995,
1996, 1997
by Jove Publications, Inc.
This book may not be reproduced in whole or in part, by
mimeograph or any other means, without permission.
For information address: The Berkley Publishing Group,
200 Madison Avenue, New York, New York 10016.

The Putnam Berkley World Wide Web address is
http://www.berkley.com

ISBN: 0-515-12112-6

A JOVE BOOK®
Jove Books are published by The Berkley Publishing Group,
200 Madison Avenue, New York, New York 10016.
JOVE and the ''J'' design
are trademarks belonging to Jove Publications, Inc.

PRINTED IN THE UNITED STATES OF AMERICA

10 9 8 7 6 5 4 3 2 1

CONTENTS

MESSAGE TO LEO

Dear Leo,

Never forget how important love is, for Leo is the sign of love. It warms you, nourishes you, fills you with strength, renews your will to live. Love is life for you. You need it and feel you deserve it. Your heart demands it and your whole being emits a very real radiance when you feel love and are loving someone.

Ideally you are a passionate person, a romantic gambler with a flair for seeking and finding a love partner. It is one for your major interests, probably the most important issue in your development. Of course, everybody wants love; everybody needs it.

No matter what your birthdate is, if you're a Leo you're a lover. Male or female. Young or old. Your sex or age doesn't alter the powerful passion and drama surrounding your life. You're always ready to try a new experience and you love to flirt and play the field. If you're the boasting type, chances are your self-confidence is suffering. Sexually, when there are disappointments and confusions you tend to take them as blows to your self-image, which you like to keep as positive and optimistic as possible.

You are dashing and bold and cut a sexy figure. Proud and noble, your bearing reflects the trace of regal blood that exists somewhere in your veins. You'll gamble if you see someone you're attracted to. It excites you to be attractive to someone else and, when it's mutual, you become a knight in shining armor, a pioneer, an adventurer—a hero crossing great distances, braving real dangers, cutting through jungle after jungle, doing anything you can to be near your heart's desire. The elements of drama, danger, and high intensity prolong the life of your affairs. You delight in bringing a quality to others' lives that they cannot find anywhere else. In that sense, you must be their central source of emotional sustenance. You usually don't tolerate being second or third, and if life puts you in a position of being other than the favorite, the radiant beauty of your warm and loving personality becomes a scorching violence that can cause irreparable damage to those you love and to yourself.

You have a high sense of honor and will deny your loved one nothing. You find your joy in lighting up the lives of your chosen loved ones. You're a great provider and extend yourself to the limit to make sure that enjoyment is present in your affairs and that no whim or idea need be curtailed for lack of adequate funds or means. Pleasure, relaxation, and fun are basic elements of your personality, and anyone connected with you can look for these qualities. You are generous with everything you have, and are happy when you are sharing your blessings with the objects of your affection. You will buy the best gifts money can buy. You will offer vacations and trips. You will hand the Sun and Moon to anyone you love, because anything you do you want to do in the biggest, most spectacular way. You could make rash promises, sincere at the time because they are born out of love, but time and circumstances could make it difficult for you to deliver when the moment of truth comes.

Your romance and idealism are irresistible, and the brilliance and intensity of your ardent pursuit of someone is hard to turn down. You can put stars in anyone's eyes if you put your mind to it. Not only do you take a sportsman's joy in the chase, but you have the competitive nature of wanting to be a winner. Winning the game becomes your single-minded objective, and so the heart of your passion rises. As you get more determined to win, you turn on more, get more excited. Everything is magnified, including your promises. You get carried away with the feelings, the hopes, the optimism of all that is possible. You make sure the person you love won't forget you. You want love and you know how to get it.

When you don't get absolute devotion, there's trouble. If your love life's bad, there's a problem with your self-image that needs correcting. Either you lack confidence and feel guilty and undeserving of affection, or your past deeds (or devotion to your own ego) now turn around to remind you of what you must become. You are demanding and domineering, and your bossy intolerant nature is hard for many people to bear. You are stubborn and unyielding. Although you possess a profoundly loving nature, you often interpret independence in others as mutiny against yourself. When you smell mutiny, you crack down like a panicky commanding officer. You tighten your grip with a maniacal need to control and continue to be the central force. How dare anyone just go off and do what they please? What about you?

It isn't that you don't understand the need for independence. Quite the contrary. You cannot really take orders from anyone but yourself. When you find yourself in situations that require your unquestioning obedience, you are miserable. When you meet conditions that demand your loyalty, you rebel. You prefer your loyalty to be a loudly proclaimed emotion you alone have generated. You will not tolerate its legislation. Yet you expect to be the prime source of love and life for others. If they take one step in either direction without your permission, you react. Many times you compensate for this strong authoritarian streak in your personality by creating live-and-let-live situations in which you don't question other people's actions and they don't question yours. It's a kind of hands-off democracy you set up. It gives you the freedom you want to explore life as you see fit, but actually democracy is not your true philosophy. If anything, you prefer to be an enlightened despot. Grandiose, inspiring, and proud, you must ultimately grant freedom to others, for your primary desire is to have freedom yourself. Although you are a seeker of truth, your baser side may care little for justice or personal freedom, as long as you are getting all the attention you think you deserve. You squawk like an infant and spare no tirades, tantrums, or histrionics to regain attention or control. When you calm down quickly and turn the smile back on you're given what you want.

Yours is an ego trip, all right. At worst you lack integrity and will do anything, absolutely anything, for attention and to come out looking good, no matter where the blame gets placed for whatever goes wrong. In that sense you are the cowardly Lion. You fear what others will think and cannot stand to have anyone believe that you are not noble, forthright, honorable, courageous, efficient, and capable. You will resort to deviousness, ironically enough, to make sure it doesn't look like you've been devious. You can be boastful, a thoughtless show-off obsessed with covering your egocentric insecurities with a false display of bravado. Your feelings may lack depth and you can lose your emotional integrity because you get too involved with your image.

At best you are conscious of your position and never abuse it. You recognize your worth and capitalize on it. Your potentials are unlimited and you know it. You have the capacity to be a great lover and you are aware of it. You like to be depended on. You enjoy having the spotlight. You like to be admired for your talents. You love being able to offer somebody a good time. You develop yourself best as a warm, inspiring individual, positive and aggressive and filled with love, honor, and charity. The flame of adventure burns deep within your soul and you provide a strong courageous light to guide others. When courage, stamina, and constancy are called for, there you will be. When supportive lifegiving energy is needed, you are on hand to provide it.

Your strong nature and supreme will are the foundations of life for all those around you.

You love your children but may see them as reflections of yourself. You expect a lot from them and have a difficult time accepting their individuality with all their complexities and needs, their different aspects of personality. You are devastated when they make the same mistakes you made, or make what you think are unnecessary blunders. But you are all too aware of what it means to be stubborn and headstrong. You also know how vital it is for each person to get his chance to show his potential and develop the talents he thinks he has, with no interference from anybody. You don't want to cause anxiety or uncertainty in your children or to hamper their development with guilt. Yet you expect so much. Yes, you're proud to say you expect a lot. But the relationship between parent and child is one of your secret sources of sorrow.

You often have feelings of great confusion when it comes to home, family, and children. Although you are a loving, devoted parent who tries to present a good strong image for children to follow, you would often prefer them to do as you say, not as you do. As much as you love your home and family, you have to escape it at the same time. You want your home and family to be the best examples of happiness and success that your friends can peek in the window and see. You pride yourself in your children and your relationships and want your marriage to be filled with love, respect, and joy. Your home reflects the glow of your success and you are proud of it.

But you still escape from them all. Why? What is this nagging fear you have of being dependent on a family? Time and time again you'll go off, running away either geographically or mentally, only to be drawn back again by irreconcilable conflicts, guilt, worries, and inexorable responsibilities. Your self-image depends largely on your projection of yourself as the courageous, independent Lion, out on his or her own for the first time. There is a newness to your approach, a youthful vigor and fresh-hatched quality that implies you have left home behind. You detest being thought of as dependent or attached to anybody's apron strings. And so you'll assert yourself time and again to affirm your statement of individuality and selfhood. Your own childhood and your attitude toward it, your own relationship to your parents, are often tinged with bitter-sweet sorrow.

You're a sucker for flattery, so watch out. But the truth is, your talents are almost unlimited. If you're not doing something with all your potential, you'll find someone to blame, to be sure. Since failure is a concept you cannot accept, you must find a suitable place to look for responsibility. Either your parents were too strict or they weren't strict enough, or some obligation or responsibility did this or that to you, or whatever. Actually, you are more the master of your own destiny than most people around you. At some point you will stand up, shake the cobwebs off your image, and get out there and show the world how it's done—bravely and responsibly.

Leo is the sign of show business and entertainment. You love to make people laugh and be happy, hyp-notizing them with the magic of theater. You have as much if not more creative talent than any artist of your day, yet you are sometimes more taken with the image of being an artist than with the commitment and dis-cipline of being one. But your sign is ruler of all forms of amusement, pleasure, and entertainment. Creativity is one of your key words. There is something shining in you. Don't be bashful about it. (You're really not bashful anyway.) It's there, it's real, and it's something unique that needs to be expressed. You're on stage all the time anyway, forever acting a leading role. But in actual theater it's hard for you to erase yourself long enough to assume the personality presented by the character in the play. Whatever this special talent is, at some point in your life it will have to come out and be recognized—maybe not by half the population of the world, although that would be nice. You want to be recognized, loved, and appreciated for the true gifts you feel you have to offer.

In your career, people naturally like you. You are charming, seductive, and persuasive when you're feeling confident. In your ruthless moments you will set the stage for disaster just so everyone can count on you. But you are a truth-seeker at heart, with a winning manner that reflects your honesty and sincerity. You're a born leader with a commanding, decisive approach that makes people listen. When you have facts and knowledge and experience to back up your enthusiasm, you can't lose.

You're a thoughtful but demanding boss, at your best when you are diplomatically frank and gently exacting. Barking orders and screaming directions may postpone but ultimately cause the mutiny you so abhor. Your extreme self-involvement will make it necessary to have helpers around. The more thoughtful you are of them, the more they'll want to do for you. Your position can be enhanced by your bold willingness to take chances and your ability to command respect. People automatically look up to you, and your firm, resolute acceptance of authority and responsibility will lead you away from the employ of others and toward your own enterprises.

Although you are a born comedian and love the spotlight, you often work behind the scenes and control even the stars who are out there performing. You can manage, manipulate, and cajole. Your talent for creating images brings you success in fields of art, entertainment, and business. You have an unmatchable talent to produce, and this must be exercised. For years you may operate by helping others, doing things for others' careers, advancing their stations, and giving of yourself for others. Your generous spirit opens your heart to those who need you, and you rarely say no. Yet eventually you must express your own talent, develop what you have to offer, make your creative emotional statement to the world.

You'll be called a bigmouthed show-off. You'll be told to pipe down. You'll be labeled a glory hound and big shot. You may have trouble in school or getting a formal education. But talent is there, not just talent to dominate and feed your all-consuming inferiority-superiority complex, but real potential to light the way for others and give joy and pleasure to the world. That quality is personal integrity.

In all your relationships with people, this will be the factor that nourishes a partnership or poisons it. You need a partner who will adore you but who will be able to deal with your childish insecurities. You need a person to stand by you and assess you honestly, not just blindly flatter your foppish vanity. You need someone who can stand apart from you when you get too bossy, someone who can understand you when nobody else does. You need a person who believes in freedom and needs a little separation once in a while. But what will inspire love the most is someone who recognizes your sense of integrity and helps you build it, giving you the old victory sign when you need it. You are you, for better or worse. You love it, actually, and you need to be proud of loving yourself. The healthier you are about enjoying that feeling of strong selfhood, the less likely you will be to beat people over the head with yourself.

It isn't just a sick narcissistic love affair between you and you. It's got to be more than vulgar egotism. It has to be a recognition of some cosmic force of light and life that you personify.

The integrity you feel as an individual is your great achievement. Express the truth of your feelings.

Michael Lutin

LEO SNEAK PREVIEW OF THE 21st CENTURY

As the last decade of the twentieth century comes to a close, planetary aspects for its final years connect you with the future. Major changes completed in 1995 and 1996 form the bridge to the twenty-first century and new horizons. The years 1997 through 1999 and into the year 2000 reveal hidden paths and personal hints for achieving your potential, your message from the planets.

Leo individuals, ruled by the Sun, are coming out of a period of obstacles, restrictions, and delays. Ahead are hope and idealism to put the past behind and to set out on a positive course. Pluto in Sagittarius late 1995 to the year 2007 is your guide. Sagittarius, a fire sign compatible with your fiery nature, symbolizes the search for truth, a love of wisdom, and, eventually, self-understanding. Pluto in Sagittarius starts uncovering the truth by impacting your emotions, sentiment, memory. It brings up issues of caring and nurturing, learning and teaching. Home life, family, and children are brought sharply into focus.

Another feature of the Sagittarius influence is education. You may be studying or inventing theory. You may be pursuing rigorous training in academia, the art scene, or the athletic arena. New ideas and techniques come easily. But what you learn cannot be limited to a small personal world or to an insulated family. Press to reach the larger community. Fire sign Sagittarius also augments the urge to travel. Have a specific goal at journey's end, or much energy and money can be wasted. Most of all, beware of wasting your unique vision in scattered starts and halts.

Saturn, planet of discipline, channels your vision. Saturn focuses energy and brings you down to earth.

Saturn rules both Capricorn and Aquarius, so its influence extends beyond the late '90s into the twenty-first century. First, no-nonsense Capricorn gets your act together from the idea and talking stage into concrete action. Capricorn sets serious goals and builds solid empires. Both the good-luck planet Jupiter in Capricorn 1996 to 1997 and the visionary planet Neptune in Capricorn till late 1998 steer you safely out of fancy's way into real opportunity and potential success.

Saturn inexorably modifies expansive Sagittarius and its ruler Jupiter as Jupiter transits the signs. Jupiter in Capricorn also gives you the executive ability to organize your own creations and to lead others in theirs. Jupiter in Capricorn naturally reinforces the emphasis on home, family, and property. Jupiter in Aquarius 1997 to early 1998 promotes professional and educational goals while protecting you from excesses of competition. Jupiter in Aries 1998 to 1999 accents creativity and innovation, and while Saturn is in Aries 1996 to 1999 forms an energetically helpful aspect to your own fiery nature. Jupiter in Taurus March 1999 to spring 2000 manages a blend of imagination and practicality that ensures success.

Airy Aquarius, your zodical mate as well as your zodiacal opposite, has important lessons as the century turns. Aquarius poses involvement in the larger community beyond self, family, friends, and associates. Uranus in Aquarius early 1996 to 2003 mutes your individualistic bent, making you more group-minded. Neptune in Aquarius late 1998 to 2011 replaces fickle impulses and irresponsible relationships with loyal and trustworthy ties. With a strong belief in social reforms and with family and friends behind you, you can be a leader in the community. The humanitarianism of Aquarius lets you reach out and be at the center of the action to make the world a better place.

THE CUSP-BORN LEO

Are you *really* a Leo? If your birthday falls during the fourth week of July, at the beginning of Leo, will you still retain the traits of Cancer, the sign of the Zodiac before Leo? What if you were born late in August—are you more Virgo than Leo? Many people born at the edge, or cusp, of a sign have difficulty determining exactly what sign they are. If you are one of these people, here's how you can figure it out, once and for all.

Consult the table on page 17. Find the year you were born, and then note the day. The table will tell you the precise days on which the Sun entered and left your sign for the year of your birth. If you were born at the beginning or end of Leo, yours is a lifetime reflecting a process of subtle transformation. Your life on Earth will symbolize a significant change in consciousness, for you are either about to enter a whole new way of living or you are leaving one behind.

If you are a Leo, born during the fourth week of July, you may want to read the horoscope book for Cancer as well as Leo. Cancer holds the keys to many of your secret uncertainties and deep-rooted problems, and your secret needs and wishes. You are the spirit of independence and creativity, or want to be. Yet through Cancer you reveal your deep, but often hidden, need to have strong ties. You may be trying to leave dependencies behind, yet you find yourself drawn again and again to the past or to family responsibilities.

You reflect the birth of a new sign, a ripe, whole person, fully able to tap and realize all your potentials for love and creativity.

If you were born after the third week of August, you may want to read the horoscope book for Virgo as well, for through Virgo you learn to put all your talents as a lover or creator to work. Your love for life is infectious, and your zest and sunny disposition are an inspiration to everyone around you. You are capable of seriousness, discipline, and great diligence.

You are a lover—ardent, passionate, and determined that love will not elude you. Though you may try to avoid it, you will find yourself in work, health, or duty situations that demand less emotion and more mind. You are not afraid of taking a gamble and are reluctant to give up your love of enjoyment for work or studies. You can blend professionalism and propriety in perfect amounts. You are the natural mixture of creativity and discipline, able to feel and to analyze.

You symbolize the warmth and fullness of a late summer day, a natural ripeness and maturity that is mellow and comfortable to be near.

THE CUSPS OF LEO

DATES SUN ENTERS LEO
(LEAVES CANCER)

July 23 every year from 1900 to 2000,
except for the following:

July 22

1928	1953	1968	1981	1992
32	56	69	84	93
36	57	72	85	94
40	60	73	86	96
44	61	76	88	97
48	64	77	89	98
52	65	80	90	

DATES SUN LEAVES LEO
(ENTERS VIRGO)

August 23 every year from 1900 to 2000,
except for the following:

August 22			August 24	
1960	1980	1992	1903	1919
64	84	93	07	23
68	88	96	11	27
72	89	97	15	
76				

LEO RISING:
YOUR ASCENDANT

Could you be a "double" Leo? That is, could you have Leo as your Rising sign as well as your Sun sign? The tables on pages 20–21 will tell you Leos what your Rising sign happens to be. Just find the hour of your birth, then find the day of your birth, and you will see which sign of the Zodiac is your Ascendant, as the Rising sign is called. For a detailed discussion on how the Rising sign is determined, see pages 82–85.

Your Ascendant, or Rising sign, modifies your basic Sun sign personality, and it affects the way you act out the daily predictions for your Sun sign. If your Rising sign indeed is Leo, what follows is a description of its effect on your horoscope. If your Rising sign is some other sign of the Zodiac, you may wish to read the horoscope book for that sign as well.

With Leo Rising the planet on the Ascendant is the Sun. Here it may give you a special robustness—in appearance, in health, in spirit, in action—that you can count on long after your normal energy reserves are spent. On the negative side the Sun here may give you an overdose of pride and insolence, making you quick to resent or retaliate when reason instead should be the response.

A flair for the dramatic will be evident in the fabric of your life. You like managing people and events as long as you can play center stage, or at least create a powerful character part. You may weave intrigue if it provides an opportunity for you to take a leading role. Although you like pulling strings, your frank and generous disposition rises above petty disputes. You abhor superficial alliances and cliques.

Drama stamps your personal appearance, your possessions, your surroundings. You may adorn yourself and your environment as much for the effect it will create as for the comfort it will provide. Your appearance itself, whether natural or affected, runs to the high, the proud, and the bold. You can use physical gestures as signals—to lure, to persuade, to threaten. And because love, especially to be loved, is a fundament of your ego, your body language acts instinctively to attract people to you.

Your search for identity is usually not solitary or introspective. Public appreciation and power are essential to you. You need constant interaction and approval. You may find the most satisfying ties with groups whose goals are humanitarian and ideological. But first you may discvoer in youth and early adulthood many facets of yourself through creative activity. It is imperative for you with Leo Rising to create—a work of art, a child, an intrigue, a love affair, a partnership, or a principle.

Your need for people may reflect an inner insecurity. Your self-image may not be actualized until you see it mirrored in people's responses; a positive one reinforces enthusiasm, a negative one induces self-pity. Your need for creation may also be tied to the building of an ego. You seek success and are very likely to get your lion's share of it through what you do in your lifetime.

Above all, love and loyalty are the key words for you with Leo Rising to root yourself in your environment. Love and loyalty motivate your simplest act, your grandest attempt. They, too, can be the cause of pain and loss. You are happiest when you love and are loved in return.

RISING SIGNS FOR LEO

Hour of Birth*	Day of Birth		
	July 22–27	**July 28–August 1**	**August 2–6**
Midnight	Taurus	Taurus	Gemini
1 AM	Gemini	Gemini	Gemini
2 AM	Gemini	Gemini	Cancer
3 AM	Cancer	Cancer	Cancer
4 AM	Cancer	Cancer	Cancer
5 AM	Leo	Leo	Leo
6 AM	Leo	Leo	Leo
7 AM	Leo	Leo; Virgo 8/1	Virgo
8 AM	Virgo	Virgo	Virgo
9 AM	Virgo	Virgo	Virgo
10 AM	Libra	Libra	Libra
11 AM	Libra	Libra	Libra
Noon	Libra	Libra; Scorpio 7/30	Scorpio
1 PM	Scorpio	Scorpio	Scorpio
2 PM	Scorpio	Scorpio	Scorpio
3 PM	Sagittarius	Sagittarius	Sagittarius
4 PM	Sagittarius	Sagittarius	Sagittarius
5 PM	Sagittarius	Capricorn	Capricorn
6 PM	Capricorn	Capricorn	Capricorn
7 PM	Capricorn; Aquarius 7/26	Aquarius	Aquarius
8 PM	Aquarius	Aquarius	Aquarius; Pisces 8/3
9 PM	Pisces	Pisces	Pisces
10 PM	Aries	Aries	Aries
11 PM	Aries; Taurus 7/26	Taurus	Taurus

*Hour of birth given here is for Standard Time in any time zone. If your hour of birth was recorded in Daylight Saving Time, subtract one hour from it and consult that hour in the table above. For example, if you were born at 9 AM D.S.T., see 8 AM above.

Hour of Birth*	Day of Birth		
	August 7–11	**August 12–17**	**August 18–24**
Midnight	Gemini	Gemini	Gemini
1 AM	Gemini	Gemini	Cancer
2 AM	Cancer	Cancer	Cancer
3 AM	Cancer	Cancer	Cancer; Leo 8/22
4 AM	Leo	Leo	Leo
5 AM	Leo	Leo	Leo
6 AM	Leo	Leo; Virgo 8/16	Virgo
7 AM	Virgo	Virgo	Virgo
8 AM	Virgo	Virgo	Virgo; Libra 8/22
9 AM	Libra	Libra	Libra
10 AM	Libra	Libra	Libra
11 AM	Libra	Libra; Scorpio 8/14	Scorpio
Noon	Scorpio	Scorpio	Scorpio
1 PM	Scorpio	Scorpio	Scorpio; Sagittarius 8/22
2 PM	Sagittarius	Sagittarius	Sagittarius
3 PM	Sagittarius	Sagittarius	Sagittarius
4 PM	Sagittarius	Capricorn	Capricorn
5 PM	Capricorn	Capricorn	Capricorn
6 PM	Capricorn	Aquarius	Aquarius
7 PM	Aquarius	Aquarius	Pisces
8 PM	Pisces	Pisces	Pisces; Aries 8/21
9 PM	Aries	Aries	Aries
10 PM	Aries; Taurus 8/11	Taurus	Taurus
11 PM	Taurus	Taurus	Gemini

*See note on facing page.

LOVE AND RELATIONSHIPS

No matter who you are, what you do in life, or where your planets are positioned, you still need to be loved, and to feel love for other human beings. Human relationships are founded on many things: infatuation, passion, sex, guilt, friendship, and a variety of other complex motivations, frequently called love.

Relationships often start out full of hope and joy, the participants sure of themselves and sure of each other's love, and then end up more like a pair of gladiators than lovers. When we are disillusioned, bitter, and wounded, we tend to blame the other person for difficulties that were actually present long before we ever met. Without seeing clearly into our own natures we will be quite likely to repeat our mistakes the next time love comes our way.

Enter Astrology.

It is not always easy to accept, but knowledge of ourselves can improve our chances for personal happiness. It is not just by predicting when some loving person will walk into our lives, but by helping us come to grips with our failures and reinforce our successes.

Astrology won't solve all our problems. The escapist will ultimately have to come to terms with the real world around him. The hard-bitten materialist will eventually acknowledge the eternal rhythms of the infinite beyond which he can see or hear. Astrology does not merely explain away emotion. It helps us unify the head with the heart so that we can become whole individuals. It helps us define what it is we are searching for, so we can recognize it when we find it.

Major planetary cycles have been changing people's ideas about love and commitment, marriage, partnerships, and relationships. These cycles have affected virtually everyone in areas of personal involvement. Planetary forces point out upheavals and transformations occurring in all of society. The concept of marriage is being totally reexamined. Exactly what the changes will ultimately bring no one can tell. It is usually difficult to determine which direction society will take. One thing is certain: no man is an island. If the rituals and pomp of wedding ceremonies must be revised, then it will happen.

Social rules are being revised. Old outworn institutions are indeed crumbling. But relationships will not die. People are putting less stress on permanence and false feelings of security. The emphasis now shifts toward the union of two loving souls. Honesty, equality, and mutual cooperation are the goals in modern marriage. When these begin to break down, the marriage is in jeopardy. Surely there must be a balance between selfish separatism and prematurely giving up.

There is no doubt that astrology can establish the degree of compatibility between two human beings. Two people can share a common horizon in life but have quite different habits or basic interests. Two others might have many basic characteristics in common while needing to approach their goals from vastly dissimilar points of view. Astrology describes compatibility based on these assumptions.

It compares and contrasts through the fundamental characteristics that draw two people together. Although they could be at odds on many basic levels, two people could find themselves drawn together again and again. Sometimes it seems that we keep being attracted to the same type of individuals. We might ask ourselves if we have learned anything from our past mistakes. The answer is that there are qualities in people that we require and thus seek out time and time again. To solve that mystery in ourselves is to solve much of the dilemma of love, and so to help ourselves determine if we are approaching a wholesome situation or a potentially destructive one.

We are living in a very curious age with respect to marriage and relationships. We can easily observe the shifting social attitudes concerning the whole institution of marriage. People are seeking everywhere for answers to their own inner needs. In truth, all astrological combinations can achieve compatibility. But many relationships seem doomed before they get off the ground. Astrologically there can be too great a difference between the goals, aspirations, and personal outlook of the people involved. Analysis of both horoscopes must and will indicate enough major planetary factors to keep the two individuals together. Call it what you will: determination, patience, understanding, love—whatever it may be, two people have the capacity to achieve a state of fulfillment together. We all have different needs and desires. When it comes to choosing a mate, you really have to know yourself. If you know the truth about what you are really looking for, it will make it easier to find. Astrology is a useful, almost essential, tool to that end.

In the next chapter your basic compatibility with each of the twelve signs of the Zodiac is generalized. The planetary vibrations between you and an individual born under any given zodiacal sign suggest much about how you will relate to each other. Hints are provided about love and romance, sex and marriage so that you and your mate can get the most out of the relationship that occupies so important a role in your life.

LEO:
YOU AND YOUR MATE

LEO—ARIES

A strong bond exists between you two. Once you have survived the wars waged by your egos, it will be hard to pry you apart emotionally. You are both idealistic, emotional creatures governed by the power of creation and the love of life. Love is your great source of energy, and you cannot thrive without it. Your capacity to love each other as well as yourselves is limitless. Self-involved and demanding, you can have storms and raging battles yet somehow remain loyal through it all. You are adventurous, passionate, and ardent. You make a very glamorous couple.

Ambitious and dynamic, you are both imbued with the fighting spirit and the joy of living that make whatever you do radiant with the strength of your combined spirit. As a team, whatever you dedicate yourselves to will no doubt be a success, provided selfishness and ego don't expand faster than your mutual understanding. Leo may play the baby for a long long time, but Aries will continue to love—tantrums, flirtations, and bossiness notwithstanding. You are usually grateful to have that strong Aries influence to help make dreams come true, and take new chances in life.

Hints for Your Aries Mate

This is a royal match, and you Leos better make sure you treat your Aries mate with every appearance, let alone act, of equally shared power. Aries will often play the prince, the minister, to your sovereign moods. But never underestimate the authority that your Aries partner holds and will wield if the relationship gets unruly. Allow Aries his or her sternness in your behalf; it will keep your partnership going in tandem longer than dramatic emotion or playful sexuality will. Speaking of the latter, you can always entice your lover on those levels, and it's good for Aries to feel the fun side of sex and the serious side of emotion. Often brusque and humorless when threatened, Aries will respond to your kittenish ways home alone after a hard day's work. If you've had an awful day, too, tell Aries so, and let your mate once again minister to your feelings, your problems, and your solutions. Take turns being the leader.

LEO—TAURUS

Truly a long-lasting possibility. More than just an endurance contest, you are the unified picture of loyalty, faithfulness, and honorable love.

You are both lusty, pleasure-oriented people. Taurus finds pleasure through earthly tastes for luxury and wealth and the best money can buy. Leo finds pleasure through the fiery joys of giving happiness to loved ones. You can provide a combined atmosphere of rigidity and warmth, wealth and coziness, moved by your need for status and security.

Worldly success and speculation will enter your relationship, for the passion and glamour that dazzle you both can be cooled by the harsh realities of financial liabilities and unexpected reversal. Though you are drawn together for sexual fulfillment, tender security, and worldly encouragement, you may find the opposite: frustration, insecurity, and discouragement. Yet you are both fortified with a sense of stamina, endurance, and strong codes of honor and loyalty. Great transformations can occur between you, eye-openers when you can see farther than you've ever seen before, understanding what you have never imagined, knowing something about the world and the universe beyond your sheltered lives.

Hints for Your Taurus Mate

As much as you honor the traditional, and as much as your Taurus mate agrees with you, you will have a more fulfilling relationship with Taurus if you explore the unfamiliar, follow an unorthodox route. Basically that means not paying too much attention to the physical things in your home life. Your union with Taurus should not be on account of material luxuries and comforts, though Taurus is always telling you how she or he likes to revel in those things. Food and sex do not have to be expensive or exotic to be imaginative. You do not need a velvet loveseat for the livingroom; a hammock or swing is where you and Taurus can share your most intimate thoughts. Find glamour in places where flirtation and peer pressure do not threaten. Book passage for two aboard a tramp steamer, if any exist, or join a collective farm where you and your Taurus mate can really get down to planting, weeding, hoeing, and harvesting.

LEO—GEMINI

You are cosmically linked and thus you have a natural attraction and the ability to have a harmonious relationship. Together you can reflect certainty, stability, enduring warmth and love, and gracious, cheerful acceptance of people. You are the marriage of creativity and intelligence and can express during the course of your relationship the blend of the conservative with the unusual.

At worst, your conflicts can bring out your flippant

game playing, perverse rebelliousness, and childish tantrums. It can be a serious war between honest commitment and superficial philandering, flagrant rule breaking and harsh, domineering authoritarianism. The more restless one becomes the more fearful of change you both grow. You can damage your partnership irreparably if you treat your partner's need for individual growth as mutiny. You can harm yourselves if you resist stability and regularity.

You need to unite regularity with change. You can excite each other sexually and emotionally and should always strive to elicit warmth and trust from each other. Yours is the growth from adolescence to maturity, from egotistical self-containment to mutual understanding and the experiencing of greater horizons.

Hints for Your Gemini Mate

This balmy union between you fire-ruled Leos and your airy Gemini mates needs constant sunshine and sultry breezes to make it work. Give up a little of your leonine aloofness, unbend to Gemini. The warmth of your confidences will arouse Gemini's curiosity which, once satisfied, turns to sympathy. Talk should be the mainstay of your relationship. You can keep that summertime romance going by always opening up to your Gemini partner. Neither pride nor pique nor privacy should hold you back from being totally free. Don't ever be afraid to show how upset you are. Gemini is splendid in an emergency. Expressing your ideas and feelings has an erotic effect on your Gemini partner, whose idea of perfect sexual communion is immediately after a gabfest. You'll have a lot of sex, and a lot of love, with this advice, for Gemini becomes haplessly ensnared with the person who shares the most of his or her inner self.

LEO—CANCER

You can provide light and warmth for the whole world. Ideally, your union combines the power and virility of the traditional heroic male with the sympathy and fertility of the traditional female. Together you have a sense of justice, candor, and honesty that keeps your relationship stable and secure. You can distribute responsibilities and cares between you, so that a constant source of love is generated between you, flowing outward to those around you. Sexually you can be a masterful combination. You are both imbued with powerful basic drives and the universal human need to feel emotional fulfillment through passionate and joyful union.

At worst, your relationship can be a sick play on insecurities, enslavement by an egotistical domineering despot, a subtle war between domestic guilt and personal control, between a strict parent and a child running away from home. To be fruitful, you must defend and support Cancer, and Cancer must quietly stand behind your decisions.

This is a highly spiritual blend of life forces, a productive possibility for happiness.

Hints for Your Cancer Mate

Like the gentle rain, the calm meandering streams of summertime, like a shaded, gradual clime, your Cancer mate is slowly warmed by your glow. A blaze of emotion, like the hot, hot sun, will simmer, seethe, and swirl your lover's emotions. After Cancer has let off the steam, she or he may retreat from you for a while. Come back again with gentle radiance. Put pride aside. Don't nurture your private hurts either, for that cold, cold sun will frost and ice the sentiments your Cancer mate is stewing about. Emotion is the area you Leos must handle with kid gloves around your Cancer partner. The rest of your relationship will fall into place easily. Focus on the things that keep you together—money, food, a sense of history. Even though you think differently about them, sharing them in your unique ways brings your past up to date, and sets the present in perspective for the future.

LEO—LEO

You both need special treatment and royal handling. Each of you needs attention and a lot of ego bolstering. Both need to feel loved, wanted, and desired for the warmth and strength of your supportive love. Role playing may interfere with togetherness in this union, for you both need to be the central power source. Ego clashes and too many similarities may make this a difficult match.

When this combination is successful, it is often because one of you is the mischief maker and one is the authority figure. When one of you remains central and stable, the other can depend on that stability, guidance and control. At worst, you can behave like two children, competing for attention, scrapping and scrambling to salvage your own precious egos.

At best, you are two loving souls, noble creatures meeting on the battlefield of love and matching desire for desire, passion for passion. You can give each other inspiration, dignity, and most of all freedom to develop your talents and express your true potentials.

If one of you was born between July 20 and August 1, prepare for a power-packed relationship. There will be new trips, new horizons, long-term changes in goals and relationships, with many wild, unexpected turns of fate. Both of you can benefit from this tremendous energy potential.

Hints for Your Leo Mate

You are attracted to each other like two moths to a flame—the same Leo flame. Yet you may be so courteous and fair with each other that neither of you ever gets close enough to the flame, or to each other, to be burned. That's good if your relationship is supposed to be on that joyous, platonic level. But if you, or one of you, want more, you'll have to search your nature deeply to do it. Humor, ease, letting be, and letting go characterize your union. Keep these, but add serious purpose. One of you has to let the other Leo know that without love and deep commitment to that love, your union is mostly stage setting that can be easily upset when a new star contends for the scene. You two veteran actors should share the hard knocks, the disappointments, the weariness and emptiness of glitter and popularity so that you can truly fulfill each other's real needs: work and love in tandem.

LEO—VIRGO

Together you are a remarkable mixture of hot and cold. You both need romance, warmth, and affection and both of you are capable of passion and fantasy. Together you have a seductive blend of crude emotion and refined sensibilities. You both need some distance from each other to regain control of your own lives. Honor and practicality color your emotional lives, and after feelings boil over and passions cool, you are better able to make decisions and put yourselves in order, putting aside manipulative rivalries.

Yours is the union of glamour and pragmatism, warm thrills and cool chills, good times and sober times, love and work. At worst, you can be the unhealthy combination of a despotic ruler and a resentful servant. At best, you symbolize the union of the creative lover and the dedicated artisan, turning your talents into tangible, useful gains.

This is primarily the marriage of love and work. When you conquer ego pride and fearful hypercriticism, you can reach a period of prosperous fulfillment in association. Together you represent maturity—the ripeness of a harvest time—and when united properly you can harvest a rich crop together and separately.

Hints for Your Virgo Mate

In general, you Leo lovers must distinguish between friskiness and peskiness with your Virgo mates. Virgo can be captivated by your loving vibes. That warm, sincere voice—use it a lot, Virgo likes to listen and learn. Those silky, pleading hands—don't paw, Virgo is fastidious. That robust, invigorating lust—don't eat too much, drink too much, or sleep too late, for Virgo is too alert, lean, and efficient to let you get away with sloppiness. Never whine with a Virgo. State your resentments in the most resolute manner. That will get your Virgo mate thinking rationally about the solutions, and will ensure that she or he is absolutely loyal to your cause. And you better show loyalty up front and in private with Virgo, otherwise you're done for. One of your natural Leo traits that always keeps Virgo happy is entertaining in public with friends, as long as you're your regal best.

LEO—LIBRA

You've got the possibility of a warm, loving, and responsive relationship. Together you can share affection, companionship, security, and financial success. Deep down, you are both friendly, harmonious people and can be considerate as well as passionate. It's a comfortable connection at best, sometimes as close as brother and sister.

You've got to contend with ego that can be revoltingly insatiable or controlling, and a superficial, calculated playfulness that can take real joy and fire out of living. You may get bored and restless. If you do, the relationship can degenerate into a meaningless interchange that skirts basic issues and problems. It can be a contest of arrogance and vanity, pomp and flattery, where you spend half your time puffing up an ego and the other half knocking it down.

At best, you are true companions, at times a little detached but friendly. You can be the perfect combination for love and marriage. You are the blend of stability and mutual support, the union of strength and weakness. When you change rude selfishness into stable, life-giving love, you will be most successful together. Strive to turn feelings of dependency into sincere consideration for your mate.

You and Your Libra Mate

You're the boss in this relationship with fair-minded Libra, who would rather have a boss than argue and call a confrontation. See that, know that, do that. Of course, if your bossiness ever gets vulgar or trite, Libra will leave you. But you Leos usually do not have to resort to street tactics. Your original jungle habitat makes you subtle, yet still able to cope with the inhabitants of the plains and the veldt. Subtlety is your best gambit with Libra. He or she likes to be lured into and out of things. But Libra is also a seasoned traveler of the open fields. Social, sociable, brilliant in company, liking a lot of gaiety and glamour, your Libra is easily won over if your whiskers are sleek, your tail high, and your mane smooth and flowing. In other words, be your brightest, most polished, gamest with your Libra partner in public. In private, you can roar. Be cuddly.

LEO—SCORPIO

You connect on deep emotional levels and can understand each other well, although you will not always agree. You are both aware of passion and desire. You both know how to survive crisis and how to emerge victorious from battle. You are connected by feeling, look up to one another, and find comfort and security in one another.

Sexually yours can be a steamy match, a hot-blooded surge of primitive drives and feelings. Though drawn to it, you cannot stand domination from each other, and your conflict will be as fierce as your passions are—when in the open. At worst, you battle for control and revenge. Jealousy, insecurity, and pain could take over this combination if you start to tap each other's strength—a ruthless power struggle that would be difficult to end once begun.

At best this is a tender loving match, filled with consideration and concern. You can help each other through crisis, nourish each other sexually and emotionally, and enrich each other's spirit. You're as primitive and powerful as love and death, and such a blend will imbue you both with the spirit of immortality. As tender as the bond between parent and child, this is a strong union, resistant to change and gifted with the power of regeneration.

Hints for Your Scorpio Mate

Keep doing with your Scorpio mate what you were fired to do when you first met him or her—warm those deep, cold, swirling undercurrents of emotion and ideology. You'll have to keep your hand in here, but unlike your Scorpio lover, don't hold your cards close to your chest. Leo is heart, and that's what Scorpio wants, even though she or he will do a thousand little things that on the surface seem rejecting or separative. Like the Sun, your own ruler, shining on the rivers and seas, shine on Scorpio. Make a fuss. Nurture with words, pats, caresses, snacks. Provide tidbits of gossip, propaganda, lofty ideas, grand plans. Then follow through when your Scorpio snaps at the bait. You must be free to follow Scorpio where your suggestions have led her or him. Don't shy away, kitteny and cute. Lions can stalk any terrain. Scorpio needs your fierce pride and unlimited courage to complete the journey.

LEO—SAGITTARIUS

You are always drawn to Sagittarius for that dreamer sparks your imagination and turns you on to your own talents. Together you can really accentuate the positive and eliminate the negative. Though you are both basically egocentric, you can develop a spirit of cooperation and mutual encouragement that can work miracles and assure you both of success. You both possess the love of life and the basic optimism that every relationship needs to grow to maturity. You are warm, generous creatures, capable of living together and yet separately, sharing tenderness and enthusiasm, helping each other develop skills with natural feeling and healthy buoyancy. You are an inspiration to each other.

At worst you can become wrapped up in your own worlds and egos, caught between selfishness and diffuse, unfocused excitement, bossy authoritarianism and permissive, unfilled meandering, indulgence and unrealistic dreams.

But at best together you can instead develop a blend of tact and candor, ingenuity and discipline, talent and wisdom. With its potentials for successfully manipulated risks, this is a high-stakes union where gambles must be taken. You join creativity, imagination, education, skill, and performance in areas of art, entertainment, publishing, learning, travel, speculation, and love itself.

Hints for Your Sagittarius Mate

Fire joins fire here. You Leos will kindle your Sagittarius mate's ideals, and vice versa. But when it comes down to bed and board, the fire may be nothing more than smoke and ashes. Who keeps the rent paid, who stocks the food supplies, who sees to it that family, friends, and neighbors get their due? These responsibilities must fall heavily on one of you flamboyant lovers. It might as well be you, Leo. Temper tantrums notwithstanding, your desire to succeed in the real world makes the dreams of your Sagittarius mate nursery rhymes in comparison. Don't neglect that nurturing aspect either, after you've done the day's work. Singing lullabys to your partner assures her or him of your love and also keeps the hopes and dreams alive. One day, when you've gotten beyond the here and now—which Sagittarius will require in a close partnership—you can go off and make those fantasies real.

LEO—CAPRICORN

At first you may think this is an unlikely combination, like moving a tropical island to the North Pole. But you two have many things in common and can bring each other to points of growth, development, and maturity. You both may fight a lot before you realize that. You'll complain about the constant demands—emotional or practical. You may encounter deadlocks or problems that will be insurmountable to younger or less mature members of your sign. You are both strong people. You like to be in control of your life. You don't like to feel that you're hardening, getting old or unattractive or over the hill. You both dislike feeling wildly out of control of your emotions and both of you are concerned with the image (or spectacle) you're making of yourself. You're ambitious, conservative people, imbued with the drive, determination, and stamina to get what you want.

When you don't get your own way, you can both turn ugly. Yet you are both honorable, constant, and desirous of doing your best and being great at whatever you do. Capricorn makes you work and points out all the unfinished tasks that you must get done in order for you to make it in the world. You turn Capricorn on, financially or sexually, and the pair can do a lot together. The relationship reflects your need to unify the hot and the cold within your own nature, to combine the passion of youth with the responsibility of a mature parent figure.

Hints for Your Capricorn Mate

You think you're shy in private, but you've seen nothing till you've seen your Capricorn mate freeze into reticence and isolation. That's where your Leo light and heat, which got you together in the first place, come right in. The big thaw is what's needed here. Usually reserved Capricorn will go for your sexual cavorting in a big way, directed solely to him or her, of course. Be sure you want the romp, for once aroused, your Capricorn lover will delight in having a tiger by the tail. Basically your relationship thrives in such intimate encounters as these. You won't have to worry much about the home, the social scene, the job. Share those burdens and joys with your Capricorn, because she or he is just as fit and just as traditional in those areas as you are. Raw love keeps you together; refinement graces it.

LEO—AQUARIUS

In the astrological scheme of things, Leo and Aquarius are zodiacal mates as well as zodiacal opposites. Both of you, being fixed signs, are stubborn. Leo looks to Aquarius for ideas, as Aquarius can view the realities of life with a broad philosophical view and maintain a progressive outlook. But Leo's high emotional pitch can frighten a detached Aquarius partner, who may resort to drastic measures.

You are perfect opposites. You join the qualities of a hot-blooded lover with the detachment of a scientist. Where one of you is well-ordered and dignified, needing stable planning and control, the other is disarrayed and ultracasual, craving spontaneity and unpredictability. Where one of you demands attention and obedience, the other turns wandering and rebellious.

But you complete each other perfectly and can symbolize the utter union and reconciliation of two opposing personalities. As long as you recognize each other's separateness, you can be joined. As long as you accept the fact that many of your partner's qualities are your qualities as well, you can welcome each other into your lives.

At worst, you can bring out cruelty and selfish domination or perverse, upsetting irresponsibility in each other. The more one becomes possessive and bossy, the further detached the partner becomes. The more one demands allegiance, the less support the other is able to give.

At best, you are the blend of a warm heart and intelligent mind. You can reflect the joys of a deep, private love and the human need for people, associations, and friendships outside the realms of usual love affairs.

Hints for your Aquarius Mate

You've found your Aquarius mate, because you've found someone as determined as you are, as up front as you are, as noble as you are, as addicted to social frills as serious purpose will allow. Think again when what you want together is a matter of private conflict! Aquarius will humor you for a while, but you won't think being kept in abeyance is so funny. So what happened to Leo? What happened to that open, game, playful lover that Aquarius always wanted? You got emotionally serious, but that's the last thing you can share with your Aquarius partner—emotions. It is you, Leo, who has to administer seriousness on a level that Aquarius can digest: pinches and dabs of strategy, spoonfuls of giving and taking, dashes of feeling. Please don't pour gusty expectations into the stew you're brewing with Aquarius. If you're patient, the partnership will cook to perfection.

LEO—PISCES

Though both your natures are warm, affectionate, and loving, you could remain strangers forever. Each of you may feel dominated and trapped, tied down and unable to take decisive actions because of your complex intertwined relationship. Actually, within each of you is a complex mixture of positive self-assurance and shy self-questioning. Together, you both blend the egomaniac with the selfless servant. You may feel under the thumb of a cruel demanding tyrant, or bound through guilt and responsibility to one who is weaker than you, helpless without you. Actually, this is the worst kind of Pisces-Leo relationship. You feed each other's feelings of total indispensability and worthless, confused incapacity. Yet you never let each other escape. You keep each other from growing strong or getting free.

At best, you are the perfect combination for creative expression. Together you blend the forces of mysticism, romance, and creativity. You can transform tortuous self-indulgence into spiritual strength. Emotionally and sexually, there's enough material there to marry and raise a family. Instead of resenting each other for what you are, try to maintain warmth. Together you have the capacity for love, generosity, passion, and tenderness—the whole spectrum of emotional feelings.

Hints for Your Pisces Mate

Even though you two agree on the big ideas, you won't agree with your Pisces mate's way of getting there. Loving mystery, which to you is just a series of clues and lures to pounce upon, your Pisces may deliver a staggeringly long list of maybes, nos, tomorrows, what ifs, on the other hands. Patience is a virtue you seldom exercise. Do so with your Pisces mate. All you are asked to sacrifice is your sense of timing. Pounce, okay, but do not prey; it's unfair for a cat to take advantage of a fish. Watch, listen, and learn. And when the big moment comes, take charge of the whole affair. You'll have a lot of practice at that, because in your union with Pisces you'll have to take charge of a lot of things from money-making, homemaking, to making dreams come true.

LEO:
YOUR PROGRESSED SUN

WHAT IS YOUR NEW SIGN

Your birth sign, or Sun sign, is the central core of your whole personality. It symbolizes everything you try to do and be. It is your main streak, your major source of power, vitality, and life. But as you live you learn, and as you learn you progress. The element in your horoscope that measures your progress is called the Progressed Sun. It is the symbol of your growth on Earth, and represents new threads that run through your life. The Progressed Sun measures big changes, turning points, and major decisions. It will often describe the path you are taking toward the fulfillment of your desires and goals.

Below you will find brief descriptions of the Progressed Sun in three signs. According to the table on page 43, find out about your Progressed Sun and see how and where you fit into the cosmic scheme. Each period lasts about 30 years, so watch and see how dramatic these changes turn out to be.

If Your Sun Is Progressing Into—

VIRGO, your sense of purpose gets more serious and you involve yourself with work in a wholehearted way. You must discipline yourself to produce, develop your talents, and perfect your crafts. You start using your head as well as your heart. You will turn toward healthier ways of living, and you will purify your life and live more simply. Your purpose becomes one of service.

LIBRA, you are graduating into the world, for now you enter into contacts with other people. You come to appreciate what others have to offer. You add diplomacy to your skills. You wish to marry, form partnerships, join your life with another. Cooperate with people and learn to assess, accept, and value them for what they really are.

SCORPIO, your passions and desires are awakened now as you cross the threshold into a world of intense and fertile creativity. Your powers of penetration will never be greater than they are during this segment of your life. Sex and sexuality become your key words and you come to understand death and life, mortality and immortality. Now you can slowly transform your entire nature so that you will be like the adult butterfly emerging from its cocoon.

HOW TO USE THE TABLE

Look for your birthday in the table on the facing page. Then under the appropriate column, find out approximately when your Progressed Sun will lead you to a new sign. From that point on, for 30 years, the thread of your life will run through that sign. Read the definitions on the preceding pages and see exactly how that life thread will develop.

For example, if your birthday is August 1, your Progressed Sun will enter Virgo around your 21st birthday and will travel through Virgo until you are 51 years old. Your Progressed Sun will then move into Libra. Reading the definitions of Virgo and Libra will tell you much about your major involvements and interests during those years.

YOUR PROGRESSED SUN

If your birthday falls on:	start looking at VIRGO at age	start looking at LIBRA at age	start looking at SCORPIO at age
July 21–23	30	60	90
24	29	59	89
25	28	58	88
26	27	57	87
27	26	56	86
28	25	55	85
29	24	54	84
30	23	53	83
31	22	52	82
August 1	21	51	81
2	20	50	80
3	19	49	79
4	18	48	78
5	17	47	77
6	16	46	76
7	15	45	75
8	14	44	74
9	13	43	73
10	12	42	72
11	11	41	71
12	10	40	70
13	9	39	69
14	8	38	68
15	7	37	67
16	6	36	66
17	5	35	65
18	4	34	64
19	3	33	63
20	2	32	62
21	1	31	61

LEO BIRTHDAYS

July 23	Max Heindel, Raymond Chandler
July 24	Amelia Earhart, Bella Abzug, Zelda Fitzgerald
July 25	Walter Brennan, Eric Hoffer
July 26	Carl Jung, Stanley Kubrick, Gracie Allen
July 27	Keenan Wynn, Mary Butterworth
July 28	Beatrix Potter, Jacqueline Onassis
July 29	William Powell, Dag Hammarskjold
July 30	Emily Bronte, Elena Blavatsky
July 31	George Baxter, Evonne Goolagong
Aug. 1	Herman Melville, Maria Mitchell
Aug. 2	Myrna Loy, James Baldwin, Helen Morgan
Aug. 3	Dolores Del Rio, Tony Bennett
Aug. 4	Percy Bysshe Shelley
Aug. 5	Neil Armstrong, Clara Bow
Aug. 6	Lucille Ball, Louella Parsons
Aug. 7	Mata Hari, Billie Burke, Anna Magnani
Aug. 8	Andy Warhol, Sylvia Sidney, Esther Williams
Aug. 9	David Steinberg
Aug. 10	Herbert Hoover, Norma Shearer
Aug. 11	Louise Bogan
Aug. 12	Cecil B. DeMille
Aug. 13	Annie Oakley, Lucy Stone
Aug. 14	John Galsworthy, Debbie Meyer
Aug. 15	Napoleon, Julia Child, Edna Ferber
Aug. 16	Ann Blyth, George Meany
Aug. 17	Davy Crockett, Mae West
Aug. 18	Shelley Winters, Virginia Dare
Aug. 19	Orville Wright, Ogden Nash, William J. Clinton
Aug. 20	Van Johnson, Jacquelline Susann
Aug. 21	Count Basie, Princess Margaret
Aug. 22	Debussy, Ray Bradbury, Dorothy Parker
Aug. 23	Louis XVI, Viva

CAN ASTROLOGY PREDICT THE FUTURE?

Can astrology really peer into the future? By studying the planets and the stars is it possible to look years ahead and make predictions for our lives? How can we draw the line between ignorant superstition and cosmic mystery? We live in a very civilized world, to be sure. We consider ourselves modern, enlightened individuals. Yet few of us can resist the temptation to take a peek at the future when we think it's possible. Why? What is the basis of such universal curiosity?

The answer is simple. Astrology works, and you don't have to be a magician to find that out. We certainly can't prove astrology simply by taking a look at the astonishing number of people who believe in it, but such figures do make us wonder what lies behind such widespread popularity. Everywhere in the world hundreds of thousands of serious, intelligent people are charting, studying, and interpreting the positions of the planets and stars every day. Every facet of the media dispenses daily astrological bulletins to millions of curious seekers. In Eastern countries, the source of many wisdoms handed down to us from antiquity, astrology still has a vital place. Why? Surrounded as we are by sophisticated scientific method, how does astrology, with all its bizarre symbolism and mysterious meaning, survive so magnificently? The answer remains the same. It works.

Nobody knows exactly where astrological knowledge came from. We have references to it dating back to the

dawn of human history. Wherever there was a stirring
of human consciousness, people began to observe the
natural cycles and rhythms that sustained their life. The
diversity of human behavior must have been evident
even to the first students of consciousness. Yet the basic similarity between members of the human family
must have led to the search for some common source,
some greater point of origin somehow linked to the
heavenly bodies ruling our sense of life and time. The
ancient world of Mesopotamia, Chaldea, and Egypt
was a highly developed center of astronomical observation and astrological interpretation of heavenly phenomena and their resultant effects on human life.

Amid the seeming chaos of a mysterious unknown
universe, people from earliest times sought to classify,
define, and organize the world around them. Order:
that's what the human mind has always striven to maintain in an unceasing battle with its natural counterpart,
chaos, or entropy. We build cities, countries, and empires, subjugating nature to a point of near defeat, and
then ... civilization collapses, empires fall, and cities
crumble. Nature reclaims the wilderness. Shelly's poem
Ozymandias is a hymn to the battle between order and
chaos. The narrator tells us about a statue, broken,
shattered, and half-sunk somewhere in the middle of a
distant desert. The inscription reads: "Look on my
works, ye mighty, and despair." And then we are told:
"Nothing beside remains. Round the decay of that co-
lossal wreck, boundless and bare, the lone and level
sands stretch far away."

People always feared the entropy that seemed to
lurk in nature. So we found permanence and constancy
in the regular movements of the Sun, Moon, and planets and in the positions of the stars. Traditions sprang
up from observations of the seasons and crops. Relationships were noted between phenomena in nature
and the configurations of the heavenly bodies. This
"synchronicity," as it was later called by Carl Jung, ex-

tended to thought, mood, and behavior, and as such developed the astrological archetypes handed down to us today.

Astrology, a regal science of the stars in the old days, was made available to the king, who was informed of impending events in the heavens, translated of course to their earthly meanings by trusted astrologers. True, astrological knowledge in its infant stages was rudimentary and beset with many superstitions and false premises. But those same dangers exist today in any investigation of occult or mystical subjects. In the East, reverence for astrology is part of religion. Astrologer-astronomers have held respected positions in government and have taken part in advisory councils on many momentous issues. The duties of the court astrologer, whose office was one of the most important in the land, were clearly defined, as early records show.

Here in our sleek Western world, astrology glimmers on, perhaps more brilliantly than ever. With all of our technological wonders and complex urbanized environments, we look to astrology even now to cut through artificiality, dehumanization, and all the materialism of contemporary life, while we gather precious information that helps us live in that material world. Astrology helps us restore balance and get in step with our own rhythms and the rhythms of nature.

Intelligent investigation of astrology (or the practical application of it) need not mean blind acceptance. We only need to see it working, see our own lives confirming its principles every day, in order to accept and understand it more. To understand ourselves is to know ourselves and to know all. This book can help you to do that—to understand yourself and through understanding develop your own resources and potentials as a rich human being.

YOUR PLACE AMONG THE STARS

Humanity finds itself at the center of a vast personal universe that extends infinitely outward in all directions. In that sense each is a kind of star radiating, as our Sun does, to all bodies everywhere. These vibrations, whether loving, helpful, or destructive, extend outward and generate a kind of "atmosphere" in which woman and man move. The way we relate to everything around us—our joy or our sorrow—becomes a living part of us. Our loved ones and our enemies become the objects of our projected radiations, for better or worse. Our bodies and faces reflect thoughts and emotions much the way light from the Sun reflects the massive reactions occurring deep within its interior. This energy and light reach all who enter its sphere of influence.

Our own personal radiations are just as potent in their own way, really. The reactions that go on deep within us profoundly affect our way of thinking and acting. Our feelings of joy or satisfaction, frustration or anger, must eventually find an outlet. Otherwise we experience the psychological or physiological repercussions of repression. If we can't have a good cry, tell someone our troubles, or express love, we soon feel very bad indeed.

As far as our physical selves are concerned, there is a direct relationship between our outer lives, inner reactions and actions, and the effects on our physical body. We all know the feeling of being startled by the sudden ring of a telephone, or the simple frustration of missing a bus. In fact, our minds and bodies are constantly reacting to outside forces. At the same time we, too, are generating actions that will cause a reaction in someone else. You may suddenly decide to phone a friend. If you are a bus driver you might speed along on your way and leave behind an angry would-be passenger. Whatever the case, mind and body are in close communication and they both reflect each other's condition. Next time you're really angry take a good long look in the mirror!

In terms of human evolution, our ability to understand, control, and ultimately change ourselves will naturally affect all of our outside relationships. Astrology is invaluable to helping us comprehend our inner selves. It is a useful tool in helping us retain our integrity, while cooperating with and living in a world full of other human beings.

Let's go back to our original question: Can astrology predict the future? To know that, we must come to an understanding of what the future is.

In simplest terms the future is the natural next step to the present, just as the present is a natural progression from the past. Although our minds can move from one to the other, there is a thread of continuity between past, present, and future that joins them together in a coherent sequence. If you are reading this book at this moment, it is the result of a real conscious choice you made in the recent past. That is, you chose to find out what was on these pages, picked up the book, and opened it. Because of this choice you may know yourself better in the future. It's as simple as that.

Knowing ourselves is the key to being able to predict and understand our own future. To learn from past experiences, choices, and actions is to fully grasp the present. Coming to grips with the present is to be master of the future.

"Know thyself" is a motto that takes us back to the philosophers of ancient Greece. Mystery religions and cults of initiation throughout the ancient world, schools of mystical discipline, yoga and mental expansion have always been guardians of this one sacred phrase. Know thyself. Of course, that's easy to say. But how do you go about it when there are so many conflicts in our lives and different parts of our personalities? How do we know when we are really "being ourselves" and not merely being influenced by the things we read or see on television, or by the people around us? How can we differentiate the various parts of our character and still remain whole?

There are many methods of classifying human beings into types. Body shapes, muscular types, blood types, and genetic types are only a few. Psychology has its own ways of classifying human beings according to their behavior. Anthropology studies human evolution as the body-mind response to environment. Biology watches physical development and adaptations in body structure. These fields provide valuable information about human beings and the ways they survive, grow, and change in their search for their place in eternity. Yet these branches of science have been separate and fragmented. Their contribution has been to provide theories and data, yes, but no lasting solutions to the human problems that have existed since the first two creatures realized they had two separate identities.

It's often difficult to classify yourself according to these different schemes. It's not easy to be objective about yourself. Some things are hard to face; others are hard to see. The different perspectives afforded to us by studying the human organism from all these different disciplines may seem contradictory when they are all really trying to integrate humankind into the whole of the cosmic scheme.

Astrology can help these disciplines unite to seek a broader and deeper approach to universal human issues. Astrology's point of view is vast. It transcends racial, ethnic, genetic, environmental, and even historical criteria, yet somehow includes them all. Astrology embraces the totality of human experience, then sets about to examine the relationships that are created within that experience.

We don't simply say, "The planets cause this or that." Rather than merely isolating cause or effect, astrology has unified the ideas of cause and effect. Concepts of past, present, and future merge and become, as we shall see a little later on, like stepping-stones across the great stream of mind. Observations of people and the environment have developed the astrological principles of planetary "influence," but it must be remembered that if there is actual influence, it is mutual. As the planets influence us, so we influence them, for we are forever joined to all past and future motion of the heavenly bodies. This is the foundation of astrology as it has been built up over the centuries.

ORDER VS. CHAOS

But is it all written in the stars? Is it destined that empires should thrive and flourish, kings reign, lovers love, and then ... decay, ruin, and natural disintegration hold sway? Have we anything to do with determining the cycles of order and chaos? The art of the true astrologer depends on his ability to uncover new information, place it upon the grid of data already collected, and then interpret what he sees as accurate probability in human existence. There may be a paradox here. If we can predict that birds will fly south, could we not, with enough time and samples for observation, determine their ultimate fate when they arrive in the south?

The paradox is that there is no paradox at all. Order and chaos exist together simultaneously in one observable universe. At some remote point in time and space the Earth was formed, and for one reason or another, life appeared here. Whether the appearance of life on planets is a usual phenomenon or an unrepeated accident we can only speculate at this moment. But our Earth and all living things upon its surface conform to certain laws of physical materiality that our observations have led us to write down and contemplate. All creatures, from the one-celled ameba to a man hurrying home at rush hour, have some basic traits in common. Life in its organization goes from the simple to the complex with a perfection and order that is both awesome and inspiring. If there were no order to our physical world, an apple could turn into a worm and cows could be butterflies.

But the world is an integrated whole, unified with every other part of creation. When nature does take an unexpected turn, we call that a mutation. This is the exciting card in the program of living experience that tells us not everything is written at all. Spontaneity is real. Change is real. Freedom from the expected norm is real. We have seen in nature that only those mutations that can adapt to changes in their environment and continue reproducing themselves will survive. But possibilities are open for sudden transformation, and that keeps the whole world growing.

FREE CHOICE AND
THE VALUE OF PREDICTIONS

Now it's time to turn our attention to the matter of predictions. That was our original question after all: Can astrology peer into the future? Well, astrological prognostication is an awe-inspiring art and requires deep philosophical consideration before it is to be undertaken. Not only are there many grids that must be laid one upon the other before such predictions can be made, but there are ethical issues that plague every student of the stars. How much can you really see? How much should you tell? What is the difference between revealing valuable data and disclosing negative or harmful programing?

If an astrologer tells you only the good things, you'll have little confidence in the analysis when you are passing through crisis. On the other hand, if the astrologer is a prophet of doom who can see nothing but the dark clouds on the horizon, you will eventually have to reject astrology because you will come to associate it with the bad luck in your life.

Astrology itself is beyond any practitioner's capacity to grasp it all. Unrealistic utopianism or gloomy determinism reflect not the truth of astrology but the truth of the astrologer interpreting what he sees. In order to solve problems and make accurate predictions, you have to be *able* to look on the dark side of things without dwelling there. You have to be able to take a look at all the possibilities, all the possible meanings of a certain planetary influence without jumping to premature conclusions. Objective scanning and assessment take much practice and great skill.

No matter how skilled the astrologer is, he cannot assume the responsibility for your life. Only you can take that responsibility as your life unfolds. In a way, the predictions of this book are glancing ahead up the road, much the way a road map can indicate turns up ahead this way or that. You, however, are still driving the car.

What, then, is a horoscope? If it is a picture of you at your moment of birth, are you then frozen forever in time and space, unable to budge or deviate from the harsh, unyielding declarations of the stars? Not at all.

The universe is always in motion. Each moment follows the moment before it. As the present is the result of all past choices and action, so the future is the result of today's choices. But if we can go to a planetary calendar and see where planets will be located two years from now, then how can individual free choice exist? This is a question that has haunted authors and philosophers since the first thinkers recorded their thoughts. In the end, of course, we must all reason things out for ourselves and come to our own conclusions. It is easy to be impressed or influenced by people who seem to know a lot more than we do, but in reality we must all find codes of beliefs with which we are the most comfortable.

But if we can stretch our imaginations up, up above the line of time as it exists from one point to another, we can almost see past, present, and future, all together. We can almost feel this vibrant thread of creative free choice that pushes forward at every moment, actually causing the future to happen! Free will, that force that changes the entire course of a stream, exists within the stream of mind itself—the collective mind, or intelligence, of humanity. Past, present, and future are mere stepping-stones across that great current.

Our lives continue a thread of an intelligent mind

that existed before we were born and will exist after we die. It is like an endless relay race. At birth we pick up a torch and carry it, lighting the way with that miraculous light of consciousness of immortality. Then we pass it on to others when we die. What we call the *unconscious* may be part of this great stream of mind, which learns and shares experiences with everything that has ever lived or will ever live on this world or any other.

Yet we all come to Earth with different family circumstances, backgrounds, and characteristics. We all come to life with different planetary configurations. Indeed each person *is* different, yet we are all the same. We have different tasks or responsibilities or lifestyles, but underneath we share a common current—the powerful stream of human intelligence. Each of us has different sets of circumstances to deal with because of the choices he or she has made in the past. We all possess different assets and have different resources to fall back on, weaknesses to strengthen, and sides of our nature to transform. We are all what we are now because of what we were before. The present is the sum of the past. And we will be what we will be in the future because of what we are now.

It is foolish to pretend that there are no specific boundaries or limitations to any of our particular lives. Family background, racial, cultural, or religious indoctrinations, physical characteristics, these are all inescapable facts of our being that must be incorporated and accepted into our maturing mind. But each person possesses the capacity for breakthrough, forgiveness, and total transformation. It has taken millions of years since people first began to walk upright. We cannot expect an overnight evolution to take place. There are many things about our personalities that are very much like our parents. Sometimes that thought makes us uncomfortable, but it's true.

It's also true that we are not our parents. You are

you, just you, and nobody else but you. That's one of the wondrous aspects of astrology. The levels on which each planetary configuration works out will vary from individual to individual. Often an aspect of selfishness will be manifested in one person, yet in another it may appear as sacrifice and kindness.

Development is inevitable in human consciousness. But the direction of that development is not. As plants will bend toward the light as they grow, so there is the possibility for the human mind to grow toward the light of integrity and truth. The Age of Aquarius that everyone is talking about must first take place within each human's mind and heart. An era of peace, freedom, and community cannot be legislated by any government, no matter how liberal. It has to be a spontaneous flow of human spirit and fellowship. It will be a magnificent dawning on the globe of consciousness that reflects the joy of the human heart to be part of the great stream of intelligence and love. It must be generated by an enlightened, realistic humanity. There's no law that can put it into effect, no magic potion to drink that will make it all come true. It will be the result of all people's efforts to assume their personal and social responsibilities and to carve out a new destiny for humankind.

As you read the predictions in this book, bear in mind that they have been calculated by means of planetary positions for whole groups of people. Thus their value lies in your ability to coordinate what you read with the nature of your life's circumstances at the present time. You have seen how many complex relationships must be analyzed in individual horoscopes before sensible accurate conclusions can be drawn. No matter what the indications, a person has his or her own life, own intelligence, basic native strength that must ultimately be the source of action and purpose. When you are living truthfully and in harmony with what you know is right, there are no forces, threats, or obstacles that can defeat you.

With these predictions, read the overall pattern and see how rhythms begin to emerge. They are not caused by remote alien forces, millions of miles out in space. You and the planets are one. What you do, they do. What they do, you do. But can you change their course? No, but you cannot change many of your basic characteristics either. Still, within that already existing framework, you are the master. You can still differentiate between what is right for you and what is not. You can seize opportunities and act on them, you can create beauty and seek love.

The purpose of looking ahead is not to scare yourself. Look ahead to enlarge your perspective, enhance your overall view of the life *you* are developing. Difficult periods cause stress certainly, but at the same time they give you the chance to reassess your condition, restate and redefine exactly what is important to you, so you can cherish your life more. Joyous periods should be lived to the fullest with the happiness and exuberance that each person richly deserves.

YOUR HOROSCOPE AND THE ZODIAC

It's possible that in your own body, as you read this passage, there exist atoms as old as time itself. You could well be the proud possessor of some carbon and hydrogen (two necessary elements in the development of life) that came into being in the heart of a star billions and billions of years ago. That star could have exploded and cast its matter far into space. This matter could have formed another star, and then another, until finally our Sun was born. From the Sun's nuclear reactions came the material that later formed the planets—and maybe some of that primeval carbon or hydrogen. That material could have become part of the Earth, part of an early ocean, even early life. These same atoms could well have been carried down to the present day, to this very moment as you read this book. It's really quite possible. You can see how everything is linked to everything else. Our Earth now exists in a gigantic universe that showers it constantly with rays and invisible particles. You are the point into which all these energies and influences have been focused. You are the prism through which all the light of outer space is being refracted. You are literally a reflection of all the planets and stars.

Your horoscope is a picture of the sky at the moment of your birth. It's like a gigantic snapshot of the positions of the planets and stars, taken from Earth. Of course, the planets never stop moving around the Sun even for the briefest moment, and you represent that motion as it was occurring at the exact hour of your birth at the precise location on the Earth where you were born.

When an astrologer is going to read your chart, he or she asks you for the month, day, and year of your birth. She also needs the exact time and place. With this information he sets about consulting various charts and tables in his calculation of the specific positions of the Sun, Moon, and stars, relative to your birthplace when you came to Earth. Then he or she locates them by means of the *Zodiac*.

The Zodiac is a group of stars, centered against the Sun's apparent path around the Earth, and these star groups are divided into twelve equal segments, or *signs*. What we are actually dividing up is the Earth's path around the Sun. But from our point of view here on Earth, it seems as if the Sun is making a great circle around our planet in the sky, so we say it's the Sun's apparent path. This twelvefold division, the Zodiac, is like a mammoth address system for any body in the sky. At any given moment, the planets can all be located at a specific point along this path.

Now where are you in this system? First you look to your *Sun sign*—the section of the Zodiac that the Sun occupied when you were born. A great part of your character, in fact the central thread of your whole being, is described by your Sun sign. Each sign of the Zodiac has certain basic traits associated with it. Since the Sun remains in each sign for about thirty days, that divides the population into twelve major character types. Of course, not everybody born the same month will have the same character, but you'll be amazed at how many fundamental traits you share with your astrological cousins of the same birth sign, no matter how many environmental differences you boast.

The dates on which the Sun sign changes will vary from year to year. That is why some people born near the *cusp*, or edge, of a sign have difficulty determining their true birth sign without the aid of an astrologer who can plot precisely the Sun's apparent motion (the Earth's motion) for any given year. But to help you find your true Sun sign, a Table of Cusp Dates for the years 1900 to 2000 is provided for you on page 17.

Here are the twelve signs of the Zodiac as western astrology has recorded them. Listed also are the symbols associated with them and the *approximate* dates when the Sun enters and exits each sign for the year 1998.

Aries	Ram	March 20–April 20
Taurus	Bull	April 20–May 21
Gemini	Twins	May 21–June 21
Cancer	Crab	June 21–July 22
Leo	Lion	July 22–August 23
Virgo	Virgin	August 23–September 23
Libra	Scales	September 23–October 23
Scorpio	Scorpion	October 23–November 22
Sagittarius	Archer	November 22–December 21
Capricorn	Sea Goat	December 21–January 20
Aquarius	Water Bearer	January 20–February 18
Pisces	Fish	February 18-March 20

In a horoscope the *Rising sign*, or Ascendant, is often considered to be as important as the Sun sign. In a later chapter (see pages 82–84) the Rising sign is discussed in detail. But to help you determine your own Rising sign, a Table of Rising Signs is provided for you on pages 20–21.

THE SIGNS OF THE ZODIAC

The signs of the Zodiac are an ingenious and complex summary of human behavioral and physical types, handed down from generation to generation through the bodies of all people in their hereditary material and through their minds. On the following pages you will find brief descriptions of all twelve signs in their highest and most ideal expression.

ARIES
The Sign of the Ram

Aries is the first sign of the Zodiac, and marks the beginning of springtime and the birth of the year. In spring the Earth begins its ascent upward and tips its North Pole toward the Sun. During this time the life-giving force of the Sun streams toward Earth, bathing our planet with the kiss of warmth and life. Plants start growing. Life wakes up. No more waiting. No more patience. The message has come from the Sun: Time to live!

Aries is the sign of the Self and is the crusade for the right of an individual to live in unimpeachable freedom. It represents the supremacy of the human will over all obstacles, limitations, and threats. In Aries there is unlimited energy, optimism, and daring, for it is the pioneer in search of a new world. It is the story of success and renewal, championship, and victory. It is the living spirit of resilience and the power to be yourself, free from all restrictions and conditioning. There is no pattern you *have* to repeat, nobody's rule you *have* to follow.

Confidence and positive action are born in Aries, with little thought or fear of the past. Life is as magic as sunrise, with all the creative potential ahead of you for a new day. Activity, energy, and adventure characterize this sign. In this sector of the Zodiac there is amazing strength, forthrightness, honesty, and a stubborn refusal to accept defeat. The Aries nature is forgiving, persuasive, masterful, and decisive.

In short, Aries is the magic spark of life and being, the source of all initiative, courage, independence, and self-esteem.

TAURUS
The Sign of the Bull

Taurus is wealth. It is not just money, property, and the richness of material possessions, but also a wealth of the spirit. Taurus rules everything in the visible world we see, touch, hear, smell, taste—the Earth, sea, and sky—everything we normally consider "real." It is the sign of economy and reserve, for it is a mixture of thrift and luxury, generosity and practicality. It is a blend of the spiritual and material, for the fertility of the sign is unlimited, and in this sense it is the mystical bank of life. Yet it must hold the fruit of its efforts in its hands and seeks to realize its fantasy-rich imagination with tangible rewards.

Loyalty and endurance make this sign perhaps the most stable of all. We can lean on Taurus, count on it, and it makes our earthly lives comfortable, safe, pleasurable. It is warm, sensitive, loving, and capable of magnificent, joyful sensations. It is conservative and pragmatic, with a need to be sure of each step forward. It is the capacity to plan around eventualities without living in the future. Steadfast and constant, this is a sturdy combination of ruggedness and beauty, gentleness and unshakability of purpose. It is the point at which we join body and soul. Unselfish friend and loyal companion, Taurus is profoundly noble and openly humanitarian. Tenacity and concentration slow the energy down to bring certain long-lasting rewards.

Taurus is a fertile resource and rich ground to grow in, and we all need it for our ideas and plans to flourish. It is the uncut diamond, symbolizing rich, raw tastes and a deep need for satisfaction, refinement, and completion.

GEMINI
The Sign of the Twins

Gemini is the sign of mental brilliance. Communication is developed to a high degree of fluidity, rapidity, fluency. It is the chance for expressing ideas and relaying information from one place to another. Charming, debonair, and lighthearted, it is a symbol of universal interest and eternal curiosity. The mind is quick and advanced, with a lightning-like ability to assimilate data.

It is the successful manipulation of verbal or visual language and the capacity to meet all events with objectivity and intelligence. It is light, quick wit, with a comic satiric twist. Gemini is the sign of writing or speaking.

Gemini is the willingness to try anything once, a need to wander and explore, the quick shifting of moods and attitudes being a basic characteristic that indicates a need for change. Versatility is the remarkable Gemini attribute. It is the capacity to investigate, perform, and relate over great areas for short periods of time and thus to connect all areas. It is mastery of design and perception, the power to conceptualize and create by putting elements together—people, colors, patterns. It is the reporter's mind, plus a brilliant ability to see things in objective, colorful arrangement. Strength lies in constant refreshment of outlook and joyful participation in all aspects of life.

Gemini is involvement with neighbors, family and relatives, telephones, arteries of news and communication—anything that enhances the human capacity for communication and self-expression. It is active, positive, and energetic, with an insatiable hunger for human interchange. Through Gemini bright and dark sides of personality merge and the mind has wings. As it flies it reflects the light of a boundless shining intellect. It is the development of varied talents from recognition of the duality of self.

Gemini is geared toward enjoying life to the fullest by finding, above all else, a means of expressing the inner self to the outside world.

CANCER
The Sign of the Crab

Cancer is the special relationship to home and involvement with the family unit. Maintaining harmony in the domestic sphere or improving conditions there is a major characteristic in this sector of the Zodiac. Cancer is attachment between two beings vibrating in sympathy with one another.

It is the comfort of a loving embrace, a tender generosity. Cancer is the place of shelter whenever there are lost or hungry souls in the night. Through Cancer we are fed, protected, comforted, and soothed. When the coldness of the world threatens, Cancer is there with gentle understanding. It is protection and understated loyalty, a medium of rich, living feeling that is both psychic and mystical. Highly intuitive, Cancer has knowledge that other signs do not possess. It is the wisdom of the soul.

It prefers the quiet contentment of the home and hearth to the busy search for earthly success and civilized pleasures. Still, there is a respect for worldly knowledge. Celebration of life comes through food. The sign is the muted light of warmth, security, and gladness, and its presence means nourishment. It rules fertility and the instinct to populate and raise young. It is growth of the soul. It is the ebb and flow of all our tides of feeling, involvements, habits, and customs.

Through Cancer is reflected the inner condition of all human beings, and therein lies the seed of knowledge out of which the soul will grow.

LEO
The Sign of the Lion

Leo is love. It represents the warmth, strength, and regeneration we feel through love. It is the radiance of life-giving light and the center of all attention and activity. It is passion, romance, adventure, and games. Pleasure, amusement, fun, and entertainment are all part of Leo. Based on the capacity for creative feeling and the desire to express love, Leo is the premier sign. It represents the unlimited outpouring of all that is warm and positive.

It is loyalty, dignity, responsibility, and command. Pride and nobility belong to Leo, and the dashing image of the knight in shining armor, of the hero, is part of Leo. It is a sense of high honor and kingly generosity born out of deep, noble love. It is the excitement of the sportsman, with all the unbeatable flair and style of success. It is a strong, unyielding will and true sense of personal justice, a respect for human freedom, and an enlightened awareness of people's needs.

Leo is involvement in the Self's awareness of personal talents and the desire and need to express them. At best it is forthrightness, courage and efficiency, authority and dignity, showmanship, and a talent for organization. Dependable and ardent, the Lion is characterized by individuality, positivism, and integrity.

It is the embodiment of human maturity, the effective individual in society, a virile creative force able to take chances and win. It is the love of laughter and the joy of making others happy. Decisive and enthusiastic, the Lion is the creative producer of the Zodiac It is the potential to light the way for others.

VIRGO
The Sign of the Virgin

Virgo is the sign of work and service. It is the symbol of the farmer at harvest time, and represents tireless efforts for the benefit of humanity, the joy of bringing the fruits of the Earth to the table of mankind. Celebration through work is the characteristic of this sign.

Sincerity, zeal, discipline, and devotion mark the sign of the Virgin.

The key word is purity, and in Virgo lies a potential for unlimited self-mastery. Virgo is the embodiment of perfected skill and refined talent. The thread of work is woven into the entire life of Virgo. All creativity is poured into streamlining a job, classifying a system, eradicating unnecessary elements of pure analysis. The true Virgo genius is found in separating the wheat from the chaff.

Spartan simplicity characterizes this sign, and Virgo battles the war between order and disorder. The need to arrange, assimilate, and categorize is great; it is the symbol of the diagnostician, the nurse, and the healer. Criticism and analysis describe this sign—pure, incisive wisdom and a shy appreciation of life's joys. All is devoted to the attainment of perfection and the ideal of self-mastery.

Virgo is the sign of health and represents the physical body as a functioning symbol of the mental and spiritual planes. It is the state of healing the ills of the human being with natural, temperate living. It is maturation of the ego as it passes from a self-centered phase to its awareness and devotion to humanity.

It is humanitarian, pragmatic, and scientific, with boundless curiosity. Focus and clarity of mind are the strong points, while strength of purpose and shy reserve underlie the whole sign. There is separateness, aloofness, and solitude for this beacon of the Zodiac. As a lighthouse guides ships, so Virgo shines.

LIBRA
The Sign of the Scales

Libra is the sign of human relationship, marriage, equality, and justice. It symbolizes the need of one human being for another, the capacity to find light, warmth, and life-giving love in relationship to another human being. It is union on any level—mental, sexual, emotional, or business. It is self-extension in a desire to find a partner with whom to share our joys. It is the capacity to recognize the needs of others and to develop to the fullest our powers of diplomacy, good taste, and refinement.

Libra is harmony, grace, aesthetic sensibility, and the personification of the spirit of companionship. It represents the skill to maintain balances and the ability to share mutually all life's benefits, trials, crises, and blessings. Libra is mastery at anticipation of another's needs or reactions. It is the exercise of simple justice with impartial delicacy.

It is the need to relate, to find a major person, place, or thing to sustain us and draw out our attention. It is growth through becoming awakened to the outside world and other people. It is the union of two loving souls in honesty, equality, mutual cooperation, and mutual accord.

SCORPIO
The Sign of the Scorpion

Scorpio is the sign of dark intensity, swirling passion, and sexual magnetism. It is the thirst for survival and regeneration that are the bases of sexual orientation and the creative impulses for self-expression. No other sign has such a profound instinct for survival and reproduction. Out of the abyss of emotions come a thousand creations, each one possessing a life of its own.

Scorpio is completion, determination, and endurance, fortified with enough stamina to outlive any enemy. It is the pursuit of goals despite any threat, warning, or obstacle that might stand in the way. It simply cannot be stopped. It knows when to wait and when to proceed. It is the constant state of readiness, a vibrant living force that constantly pumps out its rhythm from the depths of being.

Secretive and intimate, Scorpio symbolizes the self-directed creature with a will of steel. It is the flaming desire to create, manipulate, and control with a magician's touch. But the most mysterious quality is the capacity for metamorphosis, or total transformation.

This represents supremacy in the battle with dark unseen forces. It is the state of being totally fearless—the embodiment of truth and courage. It symbolizes the human capacity to face all danger and emerge supreme, to heal oneself. As a caterpillar spins its way into the darkness of a cocoon, Scorpio faces the end of existence, says goodbye to an old way of life, and goes through a kind of death—or total change.

Then, amid the dread of uncertainty, something remarkable happens. From hopelessness or personal crisis a new individual emerges, like a magnificent butterfly leaving behind its cocoon. It is a human being completely transformed and victorious. This is Scorpio.

SAGITTARIUS
The Sign of the Archer

Sagittarius is the sign of adventure and a thousand and one new experiences. It is the cause and purpose of every new attempt at adventure or self-understanding. It is the embodiment of enthusiasm, search for truth, and love of wisdom. Hope and optimism characterize this section of the Zodiac, and it is the ability to leave the past behind and set out again with positive resilience and a happy, cheerful outlook.

It is intelligence and exuberance, youthful idealism, and the desire to expand all horizons. It is the constant hatching of dreams, the hunger for knowledge, travel and experience. The goal is exploration itself.

Sagittarius is generosity, humor, and goodness of nature, backed up by the momentum of great expectations. It symbolizes the ability of people to be back in the race after having the most serious spills over the biggest hurdles. It is a healthy, positive outlook and the capacity to meet each new moment with unaffected buoyancy.

At this point in the Zodiac, greater conscious understanding begins to develop self-awareness and self-acceptance. It is an Olympian capacity to look upon the bright side and to evolve that aspect of mind we call conscience.

CAPRICORN
The Sign of the Sea Goat

Capricorn is the sign of structure and physical law. It rules depth, focus, and concentration. It is the symbol of success through perseverance, happiness through profundity. It is victory over disruption, and finds reality in codes set up by society and culture. It is the perpetuation of useful, tested patterns and a desire to protect what has already been established.

It is cautious, conservative, conscious of the passage of time, yet ageless. The Goat symbolizes the incorporation of reason into living and depth into loving.

Stability, responsibility, and fruitfulness through loyalty color this sector of the Zodiac with an undeniable and irrepressible awareness of success, reputation, and honor. Capricorn is the culmination of our earthly dreams, the pinnacle of our worldly life.

It is introspection and enlightenment through serious contemplation of the Self and its position in the world. It is mastery of understanding and the realization of dreams.

Capricorn is a winter blossom, a born professional with an aim of harmony and justice, beauty, grace, and success. It is the well-constructed pyramid: perfect and beautiful, architecturally correct, mysteriously implacable, and hard to know. It is highly organized and built on precise foundations to last and last and last. It is practical, useful yet magnificent and dignified, signifying permanence and careful planning. Like a pyramid, Capricorn has thick impenetrable walls, complex passageways, and false corridors. Yet somewhere at the heart of this ordered structure is the spirit of a mighty ruler.

AQUARIUS
The Sign of the Water Bearer

Aquarius is the symbol of idealized free society. It is the herding instinct in man as a social animal. It is the collection of heterogeneous elements of human consciousness in coherent peaceful coexistence. Friendship, goodwill, and harmonious contact are Aquarius attributes. It is founded on the principle of individual freedom and the brotherly love and respect for the rights of all men and women on Earth.

It is strength of will and purpose, altruism, and love of human fellowship. It is the belief in spontaneity and free choice, in the openness to live in a spirit of harmony and cooperation—liberated from restriction, repression, and conventional codes of conduct. It is the brilliant capacity to assimilate information instantaneously at the last minute and translate that information into immediate creative action, and so the result is to live in unpredictability.

This is the progressive mind, the collective mind—groups of people getting together to celebrate life. Aquarius is the child of the future, the utopian working for the betterment of the human race. Funds, charities, seeking better cities and better living conditions for others, involvement in great forms of media or communication, science or research in the hope of joining mankind to his higher self—this is all Aquarius.

It is invention, genius, revolution, discovery—instantaneous breakthrough from limitations. It's a departure from convention, eccentricity, the unexpected development that changes the course of history. It is the discovery of people and all the arteries that join them together. Aquarius is adventure, curiosity, exotic and alien appeal. It pours the water of life and intelligence for all humanity to drink. It is humanism, community, and the element of surprise.

PISCES
The Sign of the Fishes

Pisces is faith—undistracted, patient, all-forgiving faith—and therein lies the Pisces capacity for discipline, endurance, and stamina.

It is imagination and other-worldliness, the condition

of living a foggy, uncertain realm of poetry, music, and fantasy. Passive and compassionate, this sector of the Zodiac symbolizes the belief in the inevitability of life. It represents the view of life that everything exists in waves, like the sea. All reality as we know it is a dream, a magic illusion that must ultimately be washed away. Tides pull this way and that, whirlpools and undercurrents sweep across the bottom of life's existence, but in Pisces there is total acceptance of all tides, all rhythms, all possibilities. It is the final resolution of all personal contradictions and all confusing paradoxes.

It is the search for truth and honesty, and the devotion to love, utterly and unquestionably. It is the desire to act with wisdom, kindness, and responsibility and to welcome humanity completely free from scorn, malice, discrimination, or prejudice. It is total, all-embracing, idealistic love. It is the acceptance of two sides of a question at once and love through sacrifice.

Pisces is beyond reality. We are here today, but may be gone tomorrow. Let the tide of circumstances carry you where it will, for nothing is forever. As all things come, so must they go. In the final reel, all things must pass away. It is deliverance from sorrow through surrender to the infinite. The emotions are as vast as the ocean, yet in the pain of confusion there is hope in the secret cell of one's own heart. Pisces symbolizes liberation from pain through love, faith, and forgiveness.

THE SIGNS AND
THEIR KEY WORDS

		Positive	Negative
ARIES	self	courage, initiative, pioneer instinct	brash rudeness, selfish impetuosity
TAURUS	money	endurance, loyalty, wealth	obstinacy, gluttony
GEMINI	mind	versatility, communication	capriciousness, unreliability
CANCER	family	sympathy, homing instinct	clannishness, childishness
LEO	children	love, authority, integrity	egotism, force
VIRGO	work	purity, industry, analysis	faultfinding, cynicism
LIBRA	marriage	harmony, justice	vacillation, superficiality
SCORPIO	sex	survival, regeneration	vengeance, discord
SAGITTARIUS	travel	optimism, higher learning	lawlessness, irresponsibility
CAPRICORN	career	depth, responsibility	narrowness, gloom
AQUARIUS	friends	humanity, genius	perverse unpredictability
PISCES	faith	spiritual love, universality	diffusion, escapism

THE ELEMENTS AND
THE QUALITIES OF THE SIGNS

Every sign has both an element and a quality associated with it. The element indicates the basic makeup of the sign, and the quality describes the kind of activity associated with each.

Element	Sign	Quality	Sign
Fire	Aries Leo Sagittarius	Cardinal	Aries Libra Cancer Capricorn
Earth	Taurus Virgo Capricorn	Fixed	Taurus Leo Scorpio Aquarius
Air	Gemini Libra Aquarius	Mutable	Gemini Virgo Sagittarius Pisces
Water	Cancer Scorpio Pisces		

Signs can be grouped together according to their element and quality. Signs of the same element share many basic traits in common. They tend to form stable configurations and ultimately harmonious relationships. Signs of the same quality are often less harmonious, but share many dynamic potentials for growth and profound fulfillment.

The following pages describe these sign groupings in more detail.

The Fire Signs

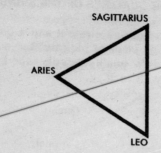

This is the fire group. On the whole these are emotional, volatile types, quick to anger, quick to forgive. They are adventurous, powerful people and act as a source of inspiration for everyone. They spark into action with immediate exuberant impulses. They are intelligent, self-involved, creative, and idealistic. They all share a certain vibrancy and glow that outwardly reflects an inner flame and passion for living.

The Earth Signs

This is the earth group. They are in constant touch with the material world and tend to be conservative. Although they are all capable of spartan self-discipline, they are earthy, sensual people who are stimulated by the tangible, elegant, and luxurious. The thread of their lives is always practical, but they do fantasize and are often attracted to dark, mysterious, emotional people. They are like great cliffs overhanging the sea, forever married to the ocean but always resisting erosion from the dark, emotional forces that thunder at their feet.

The Air Signs

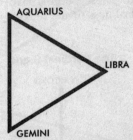

This is the air group. They are light, mental creatures desirous of contact, communication, and relationship. They are involved with people and the forming of ties on many levels. Original thinkers, they are the bearers of human news. Their language is their sense of word, color, style, and beauty. They provide an atmosphere suitable and pleasant for living. They add change and versatility to the scene, and it is through them that we can explore human intelligence and experience.

The Water Signs

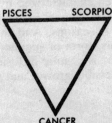

This is the water group. Through the water people, we are all joined together on emotional, nonverbal levels.

The water signs are silent, mysterious types whose magic hypnotizes even the most determined realist. They have uncanny perceptions about people and are as rich as the oceans when it comes to feeling, emotion, or imagination. They are sensitive, mystical creatures with memories that go back beyond time. Through water, life is sustained. These people have the potential for the depths of darkness or the heights of mysticism and art.

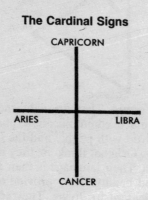

The Cardinal Signs

CAPRICORN

ARIES   LIBRA

CANCER

The cardinal signs present a picture of dynamism, activity, tremendous stress, and remarkable achievement. These people know the meaning of great change since their lives are often characterized by significant crises and major successes. The cardinal signs mark the beginning of the four seasons. And this combination is like a simultaneous storm of summer, fall, winter, and spring. The danger is chaotic diffusion of energy; the potential is irrepressible growth and victory.

The Fixed Signs

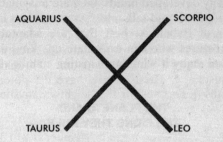

Fixed signs are always establishing themselves in a given place or area of experience. Like explorers who arrive and plant a flag, these people claim a position from which they do not enjoy being deposed. They are staunch, stalwart, upright, trusty, honorable people, although their obstinacy is well-known. Their contribution is fixity, and they are the angels who support our visible world.

The Mutable Signs

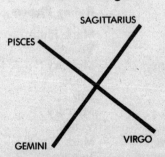

Mutable people are versatile, sensitive, intelligent, nervous, and deeply curious about life. They are the translators of all energy. They often carry out or complete tasks initiated by others. People from mutable signs have highly developed minds; they are imaginative and jumpy and think and talk a lot. At worst their lives are a Tower of Babel. At best they are adaptable and ready creatures who can assimilate one kind of experience and enjoy it while anticipating coming changes.

THE PLANETS AND THE SIGNS THEY RULE

The signs of the Zodiac are linked to the planets in the following way. Each sign is governed or ruled by one or more planets. No matter where the planets are located in the sky at any given moment, they still rule their respective signs. When they travel through the signs they rule, they have special dignity and their effects are stronger.

Following is a list of the planets and the signs they rule. After you read the definitions of the planets from pages 88 to 96, see if you can determine how the planet ruling *your* Sun sign has affected your life.

Signs	Ruling Planets
Aries	Mars, Pluto
Taurus	Venus
Gemini	Mercury
Cancer	Moon
Leo	Sun
Virgo	Mercury
Libra	Venus
Scorpio	Mars, Pluto
Sagittarius	Jupiter
Capricorn	Saturn
Aquarius	Saturn, Uranus
Pisces	Jupiter, Neptune

THE ZODIAC AND
THE HUMAN BODY

The signs of the Zodiac are linked to the human body in a direct relationship. Each sign has a part of the body with which it is associated.

It is traditionally believed that surgery is best performed when the Moon is passing through a sign *other* than the sign associated with the part of the body upon which an operation is to be performed. But often the presence of the Moon in a particular sign will bring the focus of attention to that very part of the body under medical scrutiny.

The principles of medical astrology are complex and beyond the scope of this introduction. We can, however, list the signs of the Zodiac and the parts of the human body connected with them. Once you learn these correspondences, you'll be amazed at how accurate they are.

Signs	Human Body
Aries	Head, brain, face, upper jaw
Taurus	Throat, neck, lower jaw
Gemini	Hands, arms, lungs, nerves
Cancer	Stomach, breasts, womb, liver
Leo	Heart, spine
Virgo	Intestines, liver
Libra	Kidneys, lower back
Scorpio	Sex and eliminative organs
Sagittarius	Hips, thighs, liver
Capricorn	Skin, bones, teeth, knees
Aquarius	Circulatory system, lower legs
Pisces	Feet, tone of being

THE ZODIACAL HOUSES
AND THE RISING SIGN

Apart from the month and day of birth, the exact time of birth is another vital factor in the determination of an accurate horoscope. Not only do planets move with great speed, but one must know how far the Earth has turned during the day. That way you can determine exactly where the planets are located with respect to the precise birthplace of an individual. This makes your horoscope *your* horoscope.

The horoscope sets up a kind of framework around which the life of an individual grows like wild ivy, this way and that, weaving its way around the trellis of the natal positions of the planets. The year of birth tells us the positions of the distant, slow-moving planets Jupiter, Saturn, Uranus, Neptune, and Pluto. The month of birth indicates the Sun sign, or birth sign as it is commonly called, as well as indicating the positions of the rapidly moving planets Venus, Mercury, and Mars. The day of birth, as well as the time, locates the position of our Moon. And the moment of birth—the exact hour and minute—determines the houses through what is called the Ascendant, or Rising sign.

The illustration on the next page shows the flat chart, or natural wheel, an astrologer uses. The inner circle of the wheel is labeled 1 through 12. These 12 divisions are known as the houses of the Zodiac.

The 1st house always starts from the position marked E, which corresponds to the eastern horizon. The rest of the houses 2 through 12 follow around in a "counterclockwise" direction. The point where each house starts is known as a cusp, or edge.

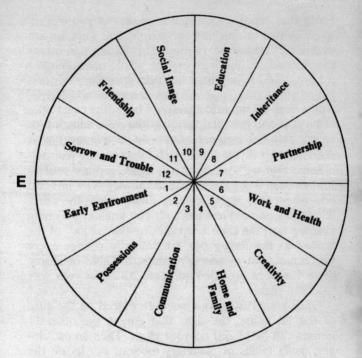

The 12 Houses of the Zodiac

The cusp, or edge, of the 1st house (point E) is where an astrologer would place your Rising sign, the Ascendant. The Rising sign is very important in a horoscope, as it defines your self-image, outlook, physical constitution, early environment, and whole orientation to life. And, as already mentioned, the exact time of your birth determines your Rising sign. Let's see how this works.

As the Earth rotates on its axis once every 24 hours, each one of the 12 signs of the Zodiac appears to be "rising" on the horizon, with a new one appearing about every two hours. Actually it is the turning of the

Earth that exposes each sign to view, but you will remember that in much of our astrological work we are discussing "apparent" motion. This Rising sign marks the Ascendant, and it colors the whole orientation of a horoscope. It indicates the sign governing the first house of the chart, and will thus determine which signs will govern all the other houses.

To visualize this idea, imagine two color wheels with twelve divisions superimposed upon each other. Just as the Zodiac is divided into twelve star groups (constellations) that we identify as the signs, another twelve-fold division is used to denote the houses. Now imagine one wheel (the signs) moving slowly while the other wheel (the houses) remains still. This analogy may help you see how the signs keep shifting the "color" of the houses as the Rising sign continues to change every two hours. But to simplify things, a Table of Rising Signs has been provided on pages 20–21 for your specific Sun sign.

Once your Rising sign has been placed on the cusp of the 1st house, the signs that govern the other 11 houses can be placed on your chart. Then an astrologer, using tables of planetary motion, can locate the positions of all the planets in their appropriate houses. The house where your Sun sign is describes your basic character and your fundamental drives. And the houses where the other planets are in your chart suggest the areas of life on Earth in which you will be most likely to focus your constant energy and center your activity.

The illustration on page 83 briefly identifies each of the 12 houses of the Zodiac. Now the pages that follow provide a detailed discussion of the meanings of the houses. In the section after the houses we will define all the known planets of the solar system, with a separate section on the Moon, in order to acquaint you with more of the astrological vocabulary you will be meeting again and again.

THE MEANING OF THE HOUSES

The twelve houses of every horoscope represent areas of life on Earth, or regions of worldly experience. Depending on which sign of the Zodiac was rising on the eastern horizon at the moment of birth, the activity of each house will be "colored" by the zodiacal sign on its cusp, or edge. In other words, the sign falling on the first house will determine what signs will fall on the rest of the houses.

1 The first house determines the basic orientation to all of life on Earth. It indicates the body type, face, head, and brain. It rules your self-image, or the way others see you because of the way you see your self. This is the Ascendant of the horoscope and is the focus of energies of your whole chart. It acts like a prism through which all of the planetary light passes and is reflected in your life. It colors your outlook and influences everything you do and see.

2 This is the house of finances. Here is your approach to money and materialism in general. It indicates where the best sources are for you to improve your financial condition and your earning power as a whole. It indicates chances for gain or loss. It describes your values, alliances, and assets.

3 This is the house of the day-to-day mind. Short trips, communication, and transportation are associated with this house. It deals with routines, brothers and sisters, relatives, neighbors, and the near environment at hand. Language, letters, and the tools for transmitting information are included in third-house matters.

4 This is the house that describes your home and home life, parents, and childhood in the sense of indicating the kind of roots you come from. It symbolizes your present home and domestic situation and reflects your need for privacy and retreat from the world, indicating, of course, what kind of scene you require.

5 Pleasure, love affairs, amusements, parties, creativity, children. This is the house of passion and courtship and of expressing your talents, whatever they are. It is related to the development of your personal life and the capacity to express feeling and enjoy romance.

6 This is the house of work. Here there are tasks to be accomplished and maladjustments to be corrected. It is the house of health as well, and describes some of the likely places where physical health difficulties may appear. It rules routines, regimen, necessary jobs as opposed to a chosen career, army, navy, police—people employed, co-workers, and those in service to others. It indicates the individual's ability to harvest the fruit of his own efforts.

7 This is the house of marriage, partnership, and unions. It represents the alter ego, all people other than yourself, open confrontation with the public. It describes your partner and the condition of partnership as you discern it. In short, it is your "take" on the world. It indicates your capacity to make the transition from courtship to marriage and specifically what you seek out in others.

8 This is the house of deep personal transition, sex as a form of mutual surrender and interchange between human beings. It is the release from tensions and the completion of the creative processes. The eighth house also has to do with taxes, inheritances, and the finances of others, as well as death as the ending of cycles and crises.

9 This is the house of the higher mind, philosophy, religion, and the expression of personal conscience through moral codes. It indicates political leanings, ethical views, and the capacity of the individual for a broader perspective and deeper understanding of himself in relation to society. It is through the ninth house that you make great strides in learning and travel to distant places and come to know yourself through study, dreams, and wide experience.

10 This is the house of career, honor, and prestige. It marks the culmination of worldly experience and indicates the highest point you can reach, what you look up to, and how high you can go in this lifetime. It describes your parents, employers, and how you view authority figures, the condition and direction of your profession, and your position in the community.

11 This is the house of friendships. It describes your social behavior, your views on humanity, and your hopes, aspirations, and wishes for an ideal life. It will indicate what kinds of groups, clubs, organizations, and friendships you tend to form and what you seek out in your chosen alliances other than with your mate or siblings. This house suggests the capacity for the freedom and unconventionality that an individual is seeking, his sense of his connection with mankind, and the definition of his goals, personal and social.

12 This is the house of seclusion, secret wisdom, and self-incarceration. It indicates our secret enemies as well, in the sense that there may be persons, feelings, or memories we are trying to escape. It is self-undoing in that this house acts against the ego in order to find a higher, more universal purpose. It rules prisons, hospitals, charities, and selfless service. It is the house of unfinished psychic business.

THE PLANETS OF THE SOLAR SYSTEM

The planets of the solar system all travel around the Sun at different speeds and different distances. Taken with the Sun, they all distribute individual intelligence and ability throughout the entire chart.

The planets modify the influence of the Sun in a chart according to their own particular natures, strengths, and positions. Their positions must be calculated for each year and day, and their function and expression in a horoscope will change as they move from one area of the Zodiac to another.

Following, you will find brief statements of their pure meanings.

THE SUN

The Sun is the center of existence. Around this flaming sphere all the planets revolve in endless orbits. Our star is constantly sending out its beams of light and energy without which no life on Earth would be possible. In astrology it symbolizes everything we are trying to become, the center around which all of our activity in life will always revolve. It is the symbol of our basic nature and describes the natural and constant thread that runs through everything that we do from birth to death on this planet.

Everything in the horoscope ultimately revolves around this singular body. Although other forces may be prominent in the charts of some individuals, still the

THE SUN

Sun is the total nucleus of being and symbolizes the complete potential of every human being alive. It is vitality and the life force. Your whole essence comes from the position of the Sun.

You are always trying to express the Sun according to its position by house and sign. Possibility for all development is found in the Sun, and it marks the fundamental character of your personal radiations all around you.

It symbolizes strength, vigor, ardor, generosity, and the ability to function effectively as a mature individual and a creative force in society. It is consciousness of the gift of life. The undeveloped solar nature is arrogant pushy, undependable, and proud, and is constantly using force.

MERCURY

Mercury is the planet closest to the Sun. It races around our star, gathering information and translating it to the rest of the system. Mercury represents your capacity to understand the desires of your own will and to translate those desires into action.

MERCURY

In other words it is the planet of mind and the power of communication. Through Mercury we develop an ability to think, write, speak, and observe—to become aware of the world around us. It colors our attitudes and vision of the world, as well as our capacity to communicate our inner responses to the outside world. Some people who have serious disabilities in their power of verbal communication have often wrongly been described as people lacking intelligence.

Although this planet (and its position in the horoscope) indicates your power to communicate your thoughts and perceptions to the world, intelligence is something deeper. Intelligence is distributed throughout all the planets. It is the relationship of the planets to each other that truly describes what we call intelligence. Mercury rules speaking, language, mathematics, draft and design, students, messengers, young people, offices, teachers, and any pursuits where the mind of man has wings.

VENUS

Venus is beauty. It symbolizes the harmony and radiance of a rare and elusive quality: beauty itself. It is refinement and delicacy, softness and charm. In astrology it indicates grace, balance, and the aesthetic sense. Where Venus is we see beauty, a gentle drawing in of energy and the need for satisfaction and completion. It is a special touch that finishes off rough edges.

VENUS

Venus is the planet of sensitivity and affection, and it is always the place for that other elusive phenomenon: love. Venus describes our sense of what is beautiful and loving. Poorly developed, it is vulgar, tasteless, and self-indulgent. But its ideal is the flame of spiritual love—Aphrodite, goddess of love, and the sweetness and power of personal beauty.

MARS

Mars is raw, crude energy. The planet next to Earth but outward from the Sun is a fiery red sphere that charges through the horoscope with force and fury. It represents the way you reach out for new adventure and new experience. It is energy drive, initiative, courage, daring. It is the power to start something and see it through. It can be thoughtless, cruel and wild, angry and hostile, causing cuts, burns, scalds, wounds. It can stab its way through a chart, or it can be the symbol of healthy spirited adventure, well-channeled constructive power to begin and keep up the drive.

MARS

If you have trouble starting things, if you lack the get-up-and-go to start the ball rolling, if you lack aggressiveness and self-confidence, chances are there's another planet influencing your Mars. Mars rules soldiers, butchers, surgeons, salespeople—in general any field that requires daring, bold skill, operational technique, or self-promotion.

JUPITER

Jupiter is the largest planet of the solar system. Planet Jupiter rules good luck and good cheer, health, wealth, optimism, happiness, success, joy. It is the symbol of opportunity and always opens the way for new possibilities in your life. It rules exuberance, enthusiasm, wisdom, knowledge, generosity, and all forms of expansion in general. It rules actors, statesmen, clerics, professional people, religion, publishing, and the distribution of many people over large areas.

♃

JUPITER

Sometimes Jupiter makes you think you deserve everything, and you become sloppy, wasteful, careless and rude, prodigal and lawless, in the illusion that nothing can ever go wrong. Then there is the danger of your showing overconfidence, exaggeration, undependability, and overindulgence.

Jupiter is the minimization of limitation and the emphasis on spirituality and potential. It is the thirst for knowledge and higher learning.

SATURN

Saturn circles our system in dark splendor with its mysterious rings, forcing us to be awakened to whatever we have neglected in the past. It will present real puzzles and problems to be solved, causing delays, obstacles, and hindrances. By doing so, Saturn stirs our own sensitivity to those areas where we are laziest.

SATURN

Here we must patiently develop method, and only through painstaking effort can our ends be achieved. It brings order to a horoscope and imposes reason just where we are feeling least reasonable. By creating limitations and boundary, Saturn shows the consequences of being human and demands that we accept the changing cycles inevitable in human life. Saturn rules time, old age, and sobriety. It can bring depression, gloom, jealousy, and greed, or serious acceptance of responsibilities out of which success will develop. With Saturn there is nothing to do but face facts. It rules laborers, stones, granite, rocks, and crystals.

THE OUTER PLANETS: URANUS, NEPTUNE, PLUTO

Uranus, Neptune, and Pluto are the outer planets. They liberate human beings from cultural conditioning, and in that sense are the lawbreakers. In early times it was thought that Saturn was the last planet of the solar system—the outer limit beyond which we could never go. The discovery of the next three planets beyond Saturn ushered in new phases of human history, revolution, and technology.

URANUS

Uranus rules unexpected change, upheaval, revolution. It is the symbol of total independence and asserts the freedom of an individual from all restriction and restraint. It is a breakthrough planet and indicates talent, originality, and genius in a horoscope. It usually causes last-minute reversals and changes of plan, unwanted separations, accidents, catastrophes, and eccentric behavior. It can add irrational rebelliousness and perverse bohemianism to a personality or a streak of unaffected brilliance in science and art.

URANUS

Uranus rules technology, aviation, and all forms of electrical and electronic advancement. It governs great leaps forward and topsy-turvy situations, and always turns things around at the last minute. Its effects are difficult to predict, since it rules sudden last-minute decisions and events that come like lightning out of the blue.

NEPTUNE

Neptune dissolves existing reality the way the sea erodes the cliffs beside it. Its effects are subtle like the ringing of a buoy's bell in the fog. It suggests a reality higher than definition can usually describe. It awakens a sense of higher responsibility often causing guilt, worry, anxieties, or delusions. Neptune is associated with all forms of escape and can make things seem a certain way so convincingly that you are absolutely sure of something that eventually turns out to be quite different.

NEPTUNE

It is the planet of illusion and therefore governs the invisible realms that lie beyond our ordinary minds, beyond our simple factual ability to prove what is "real." Treachery, deceit, disillusionment, and disappointment are linked to Neptune. It describes a vague reality that promises eternity and the divine, yet in a manner so complex that we cannot really fathom it at all. At its worst Neptune is a cheap intoxicant; at its best it is the poetry, music, and inspiration of the higher planes of spiritual love. It has dominion over movies, photographs, and much of the arts.

PLUTO

Pluto lies at the outpost of our system and therefore rules finality in a horoscope—the final closing of chapters in your life, the passing of major milestones and points of development from which there is no return. It is a final wipeout, a closeout, an evacuation. It is a subtle but powerful catalyst in all transformations that occur. It creates, destroys, then recreates. Sometimes Pluto starts its influence with a minor event or insignificant incident that might even go unnoticed. Slowly but surely, little by little, everything changes, until at last there has been a total transformation in the area of your life where Pluto has been operating. It rules mass thinking and the trends that society first rejects, then adopts, and finally outgrows.

PLUTO

Pluto rules the dead and the underworld—all the powerful forces of creation and destruction that go on all the time beneath, around, and above us. It can bring a lust for power with strong obsessions.

It is the planet that rules the metamorphosis of the caterpillar into a butterfly, for it symbolizes the capacity to change totally and forever a person's lifestyle, way of thought, and behavior.

THE MOON

Exactly how does the Moon affect us psychologically and psychically? We know it controls the tides. We understand how it affects blood rhythm and body tides, together with all the chemical fluids that constitute our physical selves. Astronauts have walked upon its surface, and our scientists are now studying and analyzing data that will help determine the age of our satellite, its origin, and makeup.

THE MOON

But the true mystery of that small body as it circles our Earth each month remains hidden. Is it really a dead, lifeless body that has no light or heat of its own, reflecting only what the gigantic Sun throws toward it? Is it a sensitive reflecting device, which translates the blinding, billowing energy from our star into a language our bodies can understand?

In astrology, the Moon is said to rule our feelings, customs, habits, and moods. As the Sun is the constant, ever shining source of life in daytime, the Moon is our nighttime mother, lighting up the night and swiftly moving, reflecting ever so rapidly the changing phases of behavior and personality. If we feel happy or joyous, or we notice certain habits and repetitive feelings that bubble up from our dark centers then vanish as quickly as they appeared, very often it is the position of the Moon that describes these changes.

THE MOON IN ALL SIGNS

The Moon moves quickly through the Zodiac, that is, through all twelve signs of our Sun's apparent path. It stays in each sign for about 2¼ days. During its brief stay in a given sign, the moods and responses of people are always colored by the nature of that sign, any planets located there at that time, or any other heavenly bodies placed in such a way that the Moon will pick up their "vibration" as well. It's astonishing to observe how clearly the Moon changes people's interests and involvements as it moves along.

The following section gives brief descriptions of the Moon's influence in each sign.

MOON IN ARIES

There's excitement in the air. Some new little thing appears, and people are quick and full of energy and enterprise, ready for something new and turning on to a new experience. There's not much patience or hesitation, doubt or preoccupation with guilty self-damning recriminations. What's needed is action. People feel like putting their plans into operation. Pleasure and adventure characterize the mood, and it's time for things to change, pick up, improve. Confidence, optimism, positive feeling pervade the air. Sick people take a turn for the better. Life stirs with a feeling of renewal. People react bravely to challenges, with a sense of courage and dynamism. Self-reliance is the key word, and people minimize their problems and maximize the power to exercise freedom of the will. There is an air of abruptness and shortness of consideration, as people are feeling the courage of their convictions to do something for themselves. Feelings are strong and intuitive, and the mood is idealistic and freedom-oriented.

MOON IN TAURUS

Here the mood is just as pleasure-loving, but less idealistic. Now the concerns are more materialistic, money-oriented, down-to-earth. The mood is stable, diligent, thoughtful, deliberate. It is a time when feelings are rich and deep, with a profound appreciation of the good things the world has to offer and the pleasures of the sensations. It is a period when people's minds are serious, realistic, and devoted to the increases and improvements of property and possessions and acquisition of wealth. There is a conservative tone, and people are fixed in their views, needing to add to their stability in every way. Assessment of assets, criticism, and the execution of tasks are strong involvements of the Taurus Moon when financial matters demand attention. It is devotion to security on a financial and emotional level. It is a fertile time, when ideas can begin to take root and grow.

MOON IN GEMINI

There is a rapid increase in movement. People are going places, exchanging ideas and information. Gossip and news travel fast under a Gemini Moon, because people are naturally involved with communication, finding out things from some, passing on information to others. Feelings shift to a mental level now, and people feel and say things that are sincere at the moment but lack the root and depth to endure much beyond the moment. People are involved with short-term engagements, quick trips. There is a definite need for changing the scene. You'll find people flirtatious and talkative, experimental and easygoing, falling into encounters they hadn't planned on. The mind is quick and active, with powers of writing and speaking greatly enhanced. Radio, television, letters, newspapers, magazines are in the spotlight with the Moon in Gemini, and new chances pop up for self-expression, with new people involved. Relatives and neighbors are tuned in to you and you to them. Take advantage of this fluidity of mind. It can rescue you from worldly involvements and get you into new surroundings for a short while.

MOON IN CANCER

Now you'll see people heading home. People turn their attention inward to their place of residence under a Cancer Moon. The active, changeable moods of yesterday vanish, and people settle in as if they were searching for a nest of security. Actually people are retiring, seeking to find peace and quiet within themselves. That's what they're feeling when they prefer to stay home rather than go out with a crowd of people to strange places. They need the warmth and comfort of the family and hearth. Maybe they feel anxious and insecure from the hustle and bustle of the workaday world. Maybe they're just tired. But it's definitely a time of tender need for emotional sustenance. It's a time for nostalgia and returning to times and places that once nourished deeply. Thoughts of parents, family, and old associations come to people. The heritage of their family ties holds them strongly now. These are personal needs that must be fed. Moods are deep and mysterious and sometimes sad. People are silent, psychic, and imaginative during this period. It's a fruitful time when people respond to love, food, and all the comforts of the inner world.

MOON IN LEO

The shift is back out in the world, and people are born again, like kids. They feel zestful, passionate, exuberant and need plenty of attention. They're interested in having a good time, enjoying themselves, and the world of entertainment takes over for a while. Places of amusement, theaters, parties, sprees, a whole gala of glamorous events, characterize this stage of the Moon's travel. Gracious, lavish hosting and a general feeling of buoyancy and flamboyance are in the air. It's a time of sunny, youthful fun when people are in the mood to take chances and win. The approach is direct, ardent, and strong. Bossy, authoritarian feelings predominate, and people throw themselves forward for all they're worth. Flattery is rampant, but the ego is vibrant and flourishing with the kiss of life, romance, and love. Speculation is indicated, and it's usually a time to go out and try your hand at love. Life is full and rich as a summer meadow, and feelings are warm.

MOON IN VIRGO

The party's over. Eyelashes are on the table. This is a time for cleaning up after the merrymakers have gone home. People are now concerned with sobering up and getting personal affairs straight, clearing up any confusions or undefined feelings from the night before, and generally attending to the practical business of doctoring up after the party. People are back at work, concerned with necessary, perhaps tedious tasks—paying bills, fixing and adjusting things, and generally purifying their lives, streamlining their affairs, and involving themselves with work and service to the community. Purity is the key word in personal habits, diet, and emotional needs. Propriety and coolness take the place of yesterday's devil-may-care passion, and the results are a detached, inhibited period under a Virgo

Moon. Feelings are not omitted; they are merely subjected to the scrutiny of the mind and thus purified. Health comes to the fore, and people are interested in clearing up problems.

MOON IN LIBRA

Here there is a mood of harmony, when people strive to join with other people in a bond of peace and justice. At this time people need relationships and often seek the company of others in a smooth-flowing feeling of love, beauty, and togetherness. People make efforts to understand other people, and though it's not the best time to make decisions, many situations keep presenting themselves from the outside to change plans and offer new opportunities. There is a general search for accord between partners, and differences are explored as similarities are shared. The tone is concilatory, and the mood is one of cooperation, patience, and tolerance. People do not generally feel independent, and sometimes this need to share or lean on others disturbs them. It shouldn't. This is the moment for uniting and sharing, for feeling a mutual flow of kindness and tenderness between people. The air is ingratiating and sometimes lacks stamina, courage, and a consistent, definite point of view. But it is a time favoring the condition of beauty and the development of all forms of art.

MOON IN SCORPIO

This is not a mood of sharing. It's driving, intense, brooding—full of passion and desire. Its baser aspects are the impulses of selfishness, cruelty, and the pursuit of animal drives and appetites. There is a craving for excitement and a desire to battle and win in a bloodthirsty war for survival. It is competitive and ruthless, sarcastic and easily bruised, highly sexual and touchy, without being especially tender. Retaliation, jealousy, and revenge can be felt too during this time. Financial involvements, debts, and property issues arise now. Powerful underworld forces are at work here, and great care is needed to transform ignorance into wisdom, to keep the mind from descending into the lower depths. During the Moon's stay in Scorpio we contact the dark undercurrents swirling around and get in touch with a magical part of our natures. Interest lies in death, inheritance, and the powers of rebirth and regeneration.

MOON IN SAGITTARIUS

Here the mind climbs out of the depths, and people are involved with the higher, more enlightened, and conscious facets of their personality. There's a renewed interest in learning, education, and philosophy, and a new involvement with ethics, morals, national and international issues: a concern with looking for a better way to live. It's a time of general improvement, with people feeling more deeply hopeful and optimistic. They are dreaming of new places, new possibilities, new horizons. They are emerging from the abyss and leaving the past behind, with their eyes gazing toward the new horizon. They decide to travel, or renew their contacts with those far away. They question their religious beliefs and investigate new areas of metaphysical inquiry. It's a time for adventure, sports, playing the field—people have their eye on new possibilities. They are bored with depression and details. They feel restless and optimistic, joyous and delighted to be alive. Thoughts revolve around adventure, travel, liberation.

MOON IN CAPRICORN

When the Moon moves into Capricorn, things slow down considerably. People require a quiet, organized, and regularized condition. Their minds are sober and realistic, and they are methodically going about bringing their dreams and plans into reality. They are more conscious of what is standing between them and success, and during this time they take definite, decisive steps to remove any obstacles from their path. They are cautious, suspicious, sometimes depressed, discouraged, and gloomy, but they are more determined than ever to accomplish their tasks. They take care of responsibilities now, wake up to facts, and wrestle with problems and dilemmas of this world. They are politically minded and concerned with social convention now, and it is under a Capricorn Moon that conditioning and conformity elicit the greatest responses. People are moderate and serious and surround themselves with what is most familiar. They want predictable situations and need time to think deeply and deliberately about all issues. It's a time for planning.

MOON IN AQUARIUS

Spontaneity replaces the sober predictability of yesterday. Now events, people, and situations pop up, and you take advantage of unsought opportunities and can expect the unexpected. Surprises, reversals, and shifts in plans mark this period. There is a resurgence of optimism, and things you wouldn't expect to happen suddenly do. What you were absolutely sure was going to happen simply doesn't. Here there is a need for adventure born from a healthy curiosity that characterizes people's moods. Unrealistic utopias are dreamed of, and it is from such idealistic dreams that worlds of the future are built. There is a renewed interest in friendship, comradeship, community, and union on high planes of mental and spiritual companionship. People free each other from grudges or long-standing deadlocks, and there is a hopeful joining of hands in a spirit of love and peace. People don't feel like sticking to previous plans, and they must be able to respond to new situations at the last minute. People need freedom. Groups of people come together and meet, perhaps for a common purpose of having dinner or hearing music, and leave knowing each other better.

MOON IN PISCES

Flashes of brilliant insight and mysterious knowledge characterize the Moon's passage in Pisces. Sometimes valuable "truths" seem to emerge which, later in the light of day, turn out to be false. This is a time of poetry, intuition, and music, when worldly realities can be the most illusory and unreliable of all. There are often feelings of remorse, guilt, or sorrow connected with a Pisces Moon—sorrow from the childhood or family or past. Confusion, anxiety, worry, and a host of imagined pains and sorrows may drag you down until you cannot move or think. Often there are connections with hospitals, prisons, alcohol, drugs, and lower forms of escape. It is a highly emotional time, when the feelings and compassion for humanity and all people everywhere rise to the surface of your being. Mysteries of society and the soul now rise to demand solutions, but often the riddles posed during this period have many answers that all seem right. It is more a time for inner reflection than positive action. It is a time when poetry and music float to the surface of the being, and for the creative artist it is the richest source of inspiration.

MOON TABLES

CORRECTION FOR NEW YORK TIME, FIVE HOURS WEST OF GREENWICH

Atlanta, Boston, Detroit, Miami, Washington, Montreal, Ottawa, Toronto, Bogota, Havana, Lima, Santiago...................... Same time

Chicago, New Orleans, Houston, Winnipeg, Churchill, Mexico City .... Deduct 1 hour

Albuquerque, Denver, Phoenix, El Paso, Edmonton, Helena....................... Deduct 2 hours

Los Angeles, San Francisco, Reno, Portland, Seattle, Vancouver .... Deduct 3 hours

Honolulu, Anchorage, Fairbanks, Kodiak... Deduct 5 hours

Nome, Samoa, Tonga, Midway .... Deduct 6 hours

Halifax, Bermuda, San Juan, Caracas, La Paz, Barbados .... Add 1 hour

St. John's, Brasilia, Rio de Janeiro, Sao Paulo, Buenos Aires, Montevideo....... Add 2 hours

Azores, Cape Verde Islands.................... Add 3 hours

Canary Islands, Madeira, Reykjavik .... Add 4 hours

London, Paris, Amsterdam, Madrid, Lisbon, Gibraltar, Belfast, Rabat .... Add 5 hours

Frankfurt, Rome, Oslo, Stockholm, Prague, Belgrade.................................... Add 6 hours

Bucharest, Beirut, Tel Aviv, Athens, Istanbul, Cairo, Cape Town, Johannesburg .... Add 7 hours

Moscow, Leningrad, Baghdad, Addis Ababa, Dhahran, Nairobi, Teheran, Zanzibar .... Add 8 hours

Bombay, Calcutta, Sri Lanka .... Add 10 ½ hours

Hong Kong, Shanghai, Manila, Peking, Perth .... Add 13 hours

Tokyo, Okinawa, Darwin, Pusan .... Add 14 hours

Sydney, Melbourne, Port Moresby, Guam ....Add 15 hours

Auckland, Wellington, Suva, Wake........... Add 17 hours

1998 MOON SIGN DATES—NEW YORK TIME

JANUARY Day Moon Enters		FEBRUARY Day Moon Enters		MARCH Day Moon Enters	
1. Aquar.		1. Aries		1. Aries	
2. Pisces	4:57 am	2. Taurus	4:26 pm	2. Taurus	0:01 am
3. Pisces		3. Taurus		3. Taurus	
4. Aries	7:44 am	4. Gemini	8:10 pm	4. Gemini	2:16 am
5. Aries		5. Gemini		5. Gemini	
6. Taurus	10:53 am	6. Gemini		6. Cancer	7:28 am
7. Taurus		7. Cancer	1:58 am	7. Cancer	
8. Gemini	2:43 pm	8. Cancer		8. Leo	3:47 pm
9. Gemini		9. Leo	9:58 am	9. Leo	
10. Cancer	7:44 pm	10. Leo		10. Leo	
11. Cancer		11. Virgo	8:10 pm	11. Virgo	2:36 am
12. Cancer		12. Virgo		12. Virgo	
13. Leo	2:46 am	13. Virgo		13. Libra	2:59 pm
14. Leo		14. Libra	8:18 am	14. Libra	
15. Virgo	0:32 pm	15. Libra		15. Libra	
16. Virgo		16. Scorp.	9:14 pm	16. Scorp.	3:52 am
17. Virgo		17. Scorp.		17. Scorp.	
18. Libra	0:45 am	18. Scorp.		18. Sagitt.	3:57 pm
19. Libra		19. Sagitt.	8:57 am	19. Sagitt.	
20. Scorp.	1:35 pm	20. Sagitt.		20. Sagitt.	
21. Scorp.		21. Capric.	5:31 pm	21. Capric.	1:44 am
22. Scorp.		22. Capric.		22. Capric.	
23. Sagitt.	0:26 am	23. Aquar.	10:11 pm	23. Aquar.	8:02 am
24. Sagitt.		24. Aquar.		24. Aquar.	
25. Capric.	7:40 am	25. Pisces	11:43 pm	25. Pisces	10:44 am
26. Capric.		26. Pisces		26. Pisces	
27. Aquar.	11:28 am	27. Aries	11:43 pm	27. Aries	10:50 am
28. Aquar.		28. Aries		28. Aries	
29. Pisces	1:09 pm			29. Taurus	10:07 am
30. Pisces				30. Taurus	
31. Aries	2:22 pm			31. Gemini	10:39 am

Summer time to be considered where applicable.

1998 MOON SIGN DATES—NEW YORK TIME

APRIL		MAY		JUNE	
Day Moon Enters		**Day Moon Enters**		**Day Moon Enters**	
1. Gemini		1. Cancer		1. Virgo	
2. Cancer	2:11 pm	2. Leo	4:50 am	2. Virgo	
3. Cancer		3. Leo		3. Libra	10:18 am
4. Leo	9:37 pm	4. Virgo	2:48 pm	4. Libra	
5. Leo		5. Virgo		5. Scorp.	11:07 pm
6. Leo		6. Virgo		6. Scorp.	
7. Virgo	8:26 am	7. Libra	3:20 am	7. Scorp.	
8. Virgo		8. Libra		8. Sagitt.	10:35 am
9. Libra	9:05 pm	9. Scorp.	4:11 pm	9. Sagitt.	
10. Libra		10. Scorp.		10. Capric.	7:51 pm
11. Libra		11. Scorp.		11. Capric.	
12. Scorp.	9:57 am	12. Sagitt.	3:49 am	12. Capric.	
13. Scorp.		13. Sagitt.		13. Aquar.	3:04 am
14. Sagitt.	9:53 pm	14. Capric.	1:40 pm	14. Aquar.	
15. Sagitt.		15. Capric.		15. Pisces	8:32 am
16. Sagitt.		16. Aquar.	9:31 pm	16. Pisces	
17. Capric.	8:06 am	17. Aquar.		17. Aries	0:24 pm
18. Capric.		18. Aquar.		18. Aries	
19. Aquar.	3:42 pm	19. Pisces	3:04 am	19. Taurus	2:48 pm
20. Aquar.		20. Pisces		20. Taurus	
21. Pisces	8:07 pm	21. Aries	6:07 am	21. Gemini	4:27 pm
22. Pisces		22. Aries		22. Gemini	
23. Aries	9:31 pm	23. Taurus	7:07 am	23. Cancer	6:40 pm
24. Aries		24. Taurus		24. Cancer	
25. Taurus	9:10 pm	25. Gemini	7:26 am	25. Leo	11:05 pm
26. Taurus		26. Gemini		26. Leo	
27. Gemini	8:56 pm	27. Cancer	8:59 am	27. Leo	
28. Gemini		28. Cancer		28. Virgo	6:55 am
29. Cancer	10:58 pm	29. Leo	1:39 pm	29. Virgo	
30. Cancer		30. Leo		30. Libra	6:06 pm
		31. Virgo	10:22 pm		

Summer time to be considered where applicable.

1998 MOON SIGN DATES—NEW YORK TIME

JULY Day Moon Enters		AUGUST Day Moon Enters		SEPTEMBER Day Moon Enters	
1. Libra		1. Scorp.		1. Capric.	
2. Libra		2. Sagitt.	2:49 am	2. Capric.	
3. Scorp.	6:46 am	3. Sagitt.		3. Aquar.	4:22 am
4. Scorp.		4. Capric.	0:19 pm	4. Aquar.	
5. Sagitt.	6:25 pm	5. Capric.		5. Pisces	7:49 am
6. Sagitt.		6. Aquar.	6:32 pm	6. Pisces	
7. Sagitt.		7. Aquar.		7. Aries	8:53 am
8. Capric.	3:28 am	8. Pisces	10:05 pm	8. Aries	
9. Capric.		9. Pisces		9. Taurus	9:17 am
10. Aquar.	9:53 am	10. Pisces		10. Taurus	
11. Aquar.		11. Aries	0:11 am	11. Gemini	10:41 am
12. Pisces	2:23 pm	12. Aries		12. Gemini	
13. Pisces		13. Taurus	2:05 am	13. Cancer	2:21 pm
14. Aries	5:46 pm	14. Taurus		14. Cancer	
15. Aries		15. Gemini	4:47 am	15. Leo	8:49 pm
16. Taurus	8:34 pm	16. Gemini		16. Leo	
17. Taurus		17. Cancer	1:56 am	17. Leo	
18. Gemini	11:19 pm	18. Cancer		18. Virgo	5:53 am
19. Gemini		19. Leo	3:02 pm	19. Virgo	
20. Gemini		20. Leo		20. Libra	4:58 pm
21. Cancer	2:44 am	21. Virgo	11:22 pm	21. Libra	
22. Cancer		22. Virgo		22. Libra	
23. Leo	7:50 am	23. Virgo		23. Scorp.	5:23 am
24. Leo		24. Libra	10:03 am	24. Scorp.	
25. Virgo	3:35 pm	25. Libra		25. Sagitt.	6:06 pm
26. Virgo		26. Scorp.	10:26 pm	26. Sagitt.	
27. Virgo		27. Scorp.		27. Sagitt.	
28. Libra	2:15 am	28. Scorp.		28. Capric.	5:31 am
29. Libra		29. Sagitt.	10:56 am	29. Capric.	
30. Scorp.	2:45 pm	30. Sagitt.		30. Aquar.	1:54 pm
31. Scorp.		31. Capric.	9:24 pm		

Summer time to be considered where applicable.

1998 MOON SIGN DATES—NEW YORK TIME

OCTOBER		NOVEMBER		DECEMBER	
Day Moon Enters		**Day Moon Enters**		**Day Moon Enters**	
1. Aquar.		1. Aries	6:28 am	1. Taurus	
2. Pisces	6:24 pm	2. Aries		2. Gemini	4:31 pm
3. Pisces		3. Taurus	6:13 am	3. Gemini	
4. Aries	7:33 pm	4. Taurus		4. Cancer	4:29 pm
5. Aries		5. Gemini	5:12 am	5. Cancer	
6. Taurus	6:58 pm	6. Gemini		6. Leo	6:56 pm
7. Taurus		7. Cancer	5:40 am	7. Leo	
8. Gemini	6:45 pm	8. Cancer		8. Leo	
9. Gemini		9. Leo	9:34 am	9. Virgo	1:22 am
10. Cancer	8:49 pm	10. Leo		10. Virgo	
11. Cancer		11. Virgo	5:38 pm	11. Libra	11:14 am
12. Cancer		12. Virgo		12. Libra	
13. Leo	2:26 am	13. Virgo		13. Libra	
14. Leo		14. Libra	4:59 am	14. Scorp.	0:17 am
15. Virgo	11:33 am	15. Libra		15. Scorp.	
16. Virgo		16. Scorp.	5:42 pm	16. Sagitt.	0:48 pm
17. Libra	11:03 pm	17. Scorp.		17. Sagitt.	
18. Libra		18. Scorp.		18. Capric.	11:56 pm
19. Libra		19. Sagitt.	6:14 am	19. Capric.	
20. Scorp.	11:37 am	20. Sagitt.		20. Capric.	
21. Scorp.		21. Capric.	5:46 am	21. Aquar.	9:18 am
22. Scorp.		22. Capric.		22. Aquar.	
23. Sagitt.	0:17 am	23. Capric.		23. Pisces	4:46 pm
24. Sagitt.		24. Aquar.	3:44 am	24. Pisces	
25. Capric.	0:06 pm	25. Aquar.		25. Aries	10:05 pm
26. Capric.		26. Pisces	11:15 am	26. Aries	
27. Aquar.	9:45 pm	27. Pisces		27. Aries	
28. Aquar.		28. Aries	3:35 pm	28. Taurus	1:06 am
29. Aquar.		29. Aries		29. Taurus	
30. Pisces	3:59 am	30. Taurus	4:54 pm	30. Gemini	2:23 am
31. Pisces				31. Gemini	

Summer time to be considered where applicable.

1998 FISHING GUIDE

	Good	Best
January	5-9-10-13-14-15-28	11-12-20
February	9-10-11-12-13-14	3-8
March	5-10-11-12-13-28	14-15-16-21
April	8-9-19	3-10-11-12-13-14-26
May	3-12-13-14-25	8-9-10-11-19
June	2-8-9-10-13-17	7-11-12-24
July	6-7-10-11-12-16-23	1-8-9-31
August	7-8-11-22-30	5-6-9-10-14
September	3-4-5-7-8-9-13-20-28	6
October	2-5-6-28	3-4-7-8-12-20
November	1-2-3-5-6-7-11-19-30	4-27
December	2-3-4-10-18-26	1-5-6

1998 PLANTING GUIDE

	Aboveground Crops	Root Crops
January	2-3-7-11-30	18-19-20-21-22-26
February	3-4-7-8-27	15-16-17-18-22-23
March	2-3-7-11-12-30	14-15-16-17-21-22-26
April	3-4-10-11-27-30	12-13-14-18-22-23
May	1-7-8-9-10-28	15-16-19-20-24
June	4-5-6-7-24-25	11-12-16-20
July	1-2-3-4-5-8-28-29-30-31	13-17-18-21-22
August	1-5-6-25-26-27-28	9-10-13-14-18
September	1-2-21-22-23-24-25-29	10-14-15
October	3-4-21-22-26-27-30-31	7-8-11-12-18-19
November	22-23-27	4-8-14-15-16-17-18
December	1-19-20-24-25-28-29	5-6-12-13-14-15

	Pruning	Weeds and Pests
January	21-22	13-14-15-16-17-23-24
February	17-18	12-13-20-21-24-25
March	16-17-26	19-20-24
April	13-14-22-23	15-16-20-21-24-25
May	19-20	12-13-17-18-22
June	16	10-13-14-18-22-23
July	13-21-22	11-15-16-19-20
August	9-10-18	8-11-12-15-16-20-21
September	14-15	8-12-16-17-18-19
October	11-12	6-9-10-13-14-15-16-17
November	8-17-18	6-10-11-12-13
December	5-6-14-15	7-8-9-10-17-18

1998 PHASES OF THE MOON—NEW YORK TIME

New Moon	First Quarter	Full Moon	Last Quarter
Dec. 29 ('97)	Jan. 5	Jan. 12	Jan. 20
Jan. 28	Feb. 3	Feb. 11	Feb. 19
Feb. 26	Mar. 5	Mar. 12	Mar. 21
Mar. 27	Apr. 3	Apr. 11	Apr. 19
Apr. 26	May 3	May 11	May 18
May 25	June 1	June 9	June 17
June 23	July 1	July 9	July 16
July 23	July 31	Aug. 7	Aug. 14
Aug. 21	Aug. 30	Sept. 6	Sept. 12
Sept. 20	Sept. 28	Oct. 5	Oct. 12
Oct. 20	Oct. 28	Nov. 4	Nov. 10
Nov. 28	Nov. 26	Dec. 13	Dec. 10
Dec. 18	Dec. 26	Jan. 1 ('99)	Jan. 9 ('99)

Each phase of the Moon lasts approximately seven to eight days, during which the Moon's shape gradually changes as it comes out of one phase and goes into the next.

There will be a partial solar eclipse during the New Moon phase on February 26 and August 21.

Use the Moon phases to connect you with your lucky numbers for this year. See the next page (page 112) and your lucky numbers.

LUCKY NUMBERS
FOR LEO: 1998

Lucky numbers and astrology can be linked through the movements of the Moon. Each phase of the thirteen Moon cycles vibrates with a sequence of numbers for your Sign of the Zodiac over the course of the year. Using your lucky numbers is a fun system that connects you with tradition.

New Moon	First Quarter	Full Moon	Last Quarter
Dec. 29 ('97)	Jan. 5	Jan. 12	Jan. 20
4 1 2 5	5 3 0 9	1 8 6 4	8 8 3 9
Jan. 28	Feb. 3	Feb. 11	Feb. 19
6 7 1 8	8 6 5 4	0 2 4 3	3 6 3 9
Feb. 26	March 5	March 12	March 21
1 4 2 3	9 8 0 5	7 7 2 8	8 5 2 3
March 27	April 3	April 11	April 19
6 4 4 1	1 0 7 9	9 4 8 5	2 8 9 3
April 26	May 3	May 11	May 18
1 8 7 0	0 4 6 1	4 5 2 6	8 9 2 1
May 25	June 1	June 9	June 17
7 6 0 5	3 5 9 4	8 1 7 8	8 2 9 4
June 23	July 1	July 9	July 16
3 0 9 2	2 6 1 7	5 4 5 8	8 6 4 2
July 23	July 31	August 7	August 14
0 8 1 5	5 9 6 0	2 4 7 5	5 3 2 1
August 21	August 30	Sept. 6	Sept. 12
8 3 5 9	4 1 7 8	3 2 9 7	7 6 0 3
Sept. 20	Sept. 28	Oct. 5	Oct. 12
3 5 1 5	2 8 9 3	6 1 8 7	7 0 4 6
Oct. 20	Oct. 28	Nov. 4	Nov. 10
6 1 8 5	2 3 6 4	4 2 1 0	0 7 9 4
Nov. 18	Nov. 26	Dec. 3	Dec. 10
4 8 8 5	6 9 7 5	2 4 0 1	1 3 7 2
Dec. 18	Dec. 26	Jan. 1 ('99)	Jan. 9 ('99)
2 8 1 2	5 3 1 9	1 0 6 8	8 3 7 4

LEO
YEARLY FORECAST: 1998

Forecast for 1998 Concerning Business
Prospects, Financial Affairs, Health,
Travel, Employment, Love and Marriage
for Persons Born with the Sun
in the Zodiacal Sign of Leo,
July 21–August 21.

This year promises to be a testing and fulfilling one for those of you born under the influence of the Sun in the zodiacal sign of Leo, whose ruler is the Sun. In several areas of life there are likely to be opportunities to expand your interests and understand more about life on a more worldly level. You should have your fair share of luck this year, in fact rather the lion's share, as befits your sign. It will be a year for taking the bull by the horns and finally getting around to tackling ventures that have previously seemed out of your reach. It is important, nonetheless, that you do not take on more than you can handle at any one time. You are likely to benefit by streamlining your endeavors so that you have sufficient time and energy to really make a go of each new venture. Where business matters are concerned, you will find that a number of new doors open to you. One particular, ongoing business interest is likely to be able to be considerably expanded. As you enter into fresh realms and tread new pastures, there should be a sense of hope and excitement. More freedom where spending is concerned in relation to professional interests is likely to mean that you can afford better equipment or training, which will most probably be a sound, long-term investment. Where your personal finances are concerned, it will be a good idea to try to build on savings this year if you can. A tightening up of your budget, especially where luxury spending is concerned, should benefit you in the long run and perhaps even more quickly than you think. In regard to health, increased physical activity, including exercise, can help to raise your energy levels and improve general fitness. It will be important, however, to seek professional advice if you are undertaking a strenuous program. Where travel is concerned, you may not find it easy to fit in as many leisure trips as you would like. But this does not mean you will not travel much this year. Indeed, you may be traveling more than usual in connection with your professional life. In regard to routine occupational affairs, the more effort you put into getting your houses in order this year, the better. There are likely to be puzzles to solve and loose ends to tie up much of the time. The clearer your decks are from the start, the easier it will be to resolve difficulties as they arise. Where love and marriage are concerned, you may not feel as certain as you have done in previous years as to your motives for being in the relationship. Unexpected occurrences are likely to help put you back on track. It is likely to be important for you and your partner to give each other plenty of space this year. If you are unattached, finding the right person may not be as difficult as you think.

Professional Leo people will find that this year will bring new opportunities for expansion. Hard work put in during the past is likely to pay off in various, perhaps unexpected ways. The enthusiasm of both colleagues and staff is likely to be an added bonus, particularly as you try to branch out into new fields. Even though several fresh interests are likely to beckon to you, it will be important to have enough time and energy to devote to each one. It is likely to be better to concentrate your energies on a few important projects than to try to spread yourself around a great deal. Individuals and companies based abroad are likely to be a help to you if you are attempting to expand overseas. This is one area where it is likely to be worth the effort you put in, trying to develop more solid contacts. Whatever you begin as a new venture this year, it will be a good idea to stick with it, even though the going can get a little rough at times. Both faith and stamina are likely to be important if you are to see positive results overall. It is best to be well prepared when you need to meet to discuss matters with authorities, particularly if legal issues are at stake. Good preparation all around is likely to bring good results, especially when you are considering the practical implications of entering into new ventures. Development time in particular needs to be taken into account. Avoid making rash financial moves during the period between May 25 and July 6.

Where personal finances are concerned, it will be a good idea this year to try to save more. This may mean having to streamline your spending, particularly when it comes to social activities or items for the home which are not really essential. Scrimping and scraping may not appeal much to your generous Leo nature, but this year you are likely to feel that you need to create more security. Besides, it may not take you as long to build up a nest egg as you imagine. Extra material and financial benefits may come your way through a partner's career success or inheritance. This should be viewed as a short-term bonus though, as far as you are concerned. In fact, a partner's tendency to be reckless where spending is concerned can potentially have adverse effects on your own security. You may feel it necessary to keep a more than usually watchful eye on your joint budget. It will not be a good idea to rely on a salary increase occurring this year even if your efforts merit one. It may be the case that the company budget cannot accommodate employee pay raises. When doing your financial planning, budget around money that you know will definitely be coming in, to be on the safe side.

Where health matters are concerned, increasing the amount of physical activity you have in a day is likely to be helpful for general fitness and possibly for a specific problem related to being too sedentary. It will be advisable to seek professional guidance before you undertake a new exercise program, especially if you are old or infirm. Mental relaxation can be an aid to general well-being, particularly if you are involved in a stressful job on a day-to-day basis. Try to avoid working for long periods without a break, as this will only increase the stress factor. Aim to keep your focus on building stamina and endurance. A healthy diet together with exercise well suited to your constitution will help to keep you in shape. Breaking clear away from your working environment at weekends also is likely to be good for you.

Where travel is concerned, this year may bring increased opportunities to travel, but these are likely to be related to work matters first and foremost. That being the case, you may not have as much time as you would like on business trips to enjoy your destination for all it has to offer. Nevertheless, glimpses of other states or countries can inspire you to want to visit more as a tourist at some time in the future. Business travel may break into your personal time on occasion. Because of this, it will be a good idea to seek out the most comfortable and relaxing travel arrangements and schedule meetings within the time you have been given. If company expenses will allow for upgraded airline seats, so much the better. In terms of personal or family vacations, it is likely to be in your interest to arrange an early break this year, preferably between February 5 and April 13. Later in the year you may find it hard to tear yourself away from your other involvements.

Where routine occupational affairs are concerned, this will be a key year for reorganization. Very old files can probably be discarded, offering up more space for the careful arrangement of new material. You may feel that a lot of your time is taken up with sorting out loose ends and other people's problems. However, your efforts are not likely to be in vain. There is likely to be a lot of satisfaction simply in getting what have seemed to be age-old difficulties and debris out of the way. Keeping your mind firmly on the task at hand can be tricky at work this year, since your concentration is likely to have a tendency to waver much more than usual. It will be a good idea to set yourself rigid schedules to stick to and write yourself notes regarding important tasks and errands which really should not be overlooked. If you can manage to take care of whatever usually ends up being neglected, it is likely that you will feel more on top of the situation overall.

Where love and marriage are concerned, you may feel a little lost in your key relationship this year. This will not necessarily be a sign that there are problems in the relationship itself, but perhaps that you both need to get back in touch with who you are and why you got together in the first place. Married Leo men and women are advised to look straight in the face issues that you find mutually difficult to discuss with your spouse. The more frank you can be with each other, the more likely you will be able to resolve any problems that have been growing between you. The very beginning of the year, until early February, will be an excellent time for forgiving and forgetting. Together you can fulfill a much prized dream. You unattached Leo people should find your faith in love restored this year. Romance is most likely to come your way when you least expect it.

LEO
DAILY FORECAST: 1998

1st Week/January 1–7

Thursday January 1st. This should be a very happy start to a new year. Surrounded by children and loved ones, you can feel expansive, generous, and happy. Playing games of skill, doing crossword puzzles, having cheerful conversation, all will pass the day pleasantly. You can have some very philosophical conversations with a mate or spouse.

Friday the 2nd. There seems to be some sort of worry with a joint money matter. You may be bothered about a tax or insurance problem that needs sorting out. You and a partner may decide to make a will. All this can cast a cloud on your pleasure. A child may be in an emotionally unhappy state. You may try to control someone's life too much.

Saturday the 3rd. Watch what you say, as you can really put your foot in it and give away a secret. Business plans don't seem to be working too well. No one seems to be too clear about the direction things are moving in. You will be wise to wait before signing an agreement. It may be too broadly worded and vague. Query any details that have been left out.

Sunday the 4th. Now it may seem a lot easier to understand what is going on around you. You are likely to be very sensitive about some financial arrangement. It may be the wisest course to work from sheer intuition. Later in the day, you and a mate or spouse may get ready for a trip some distance away. You may have a lot of organizing to do and things to prepare.

Monday the 5th. Although you can feel a bit ill, you will be determined to soldier on. People you meet on your travels can be interesting to talk to. You may find that duty calls you away from pleasure. A sick child can need your attention. Some big decisions may have to be made by you and a partner. Be sure to talk everything through with care.

Tuesday the 6th. Some of you may suffer from sea or air sickness if traveling. Get well stocked up with pills. The morning can be a chaotic time for travelers. Be careful not to get lost if in a strange area. A sense of humor will help you to get through the afternoon's odd happenings. Someone you love may be acting quite out of character.

Wednesday the 7th. You may make a bit of a scene in public if someone makes you hopping mad. You certainly don't lack courage in a stressful situation. In fact, you can be devastating. A situation at work may require you to take charge and make a decision. Don't let impulse rule you. Consider all the facts and other people's opinions. Otherwise, you may be accused of being too bossy.

Weekly Summary

You will start off the year on good terms with a mate or spouse. Even business relationships are likely to flourish. A good-humored attitude plus a willingness to be tolerant and broad-minded can help to establish good rapport with others. New Year's Day will be spent most enjoyably with relatives and loved ones around you.

You will be plunged right in the thick of it all as far as corporate or joint financial matters are concerned. There may be a query about taxes or an insurance policy. Things just don't seem too clear, and you will get a bit anxious at times. However, be patient and eventually the fog will lift and things will sort out. However, you would be wise not to rush into any agreements or sign any contracts. Be sure that all is aboveboard.

Those of you who are planning a trip overseas can have a lot of arrangements to make in advance. You may have to travel for work purposes rather than for pleasure. Some of you may also have to make a journey to fulfill a particular duty or obligation of some sort. You may not be too happy about it all, but you will be prepared to make whatever sacrifices are needed.

2nd Week/January 8–14

Thursday the 8th. Your more sensitive approach to a professional situation can really save the day. The morning can be quite an inspired time for those working in the theater or film industry. You can have a healing effect on a sick person or a small animal. The evening is likely to be spent pleasantly with a mate or spouse. You can enjoy a party or dinner date.

Friday the 9th. A formal function may turn out to be more lively than expected. You will feel very much in control of things in a group meeting later in the day. Someone may try to be difficult, but you appear to know just how to deal with this quite coolly. The day will be good for organizing social activities. An older person may ask you around for a chat.

Saturday the 10th. Things will be flowing well between you and your partner now. In fact, this will be a very happy and romantic day for you Leo people. Even staid married couples can feel as if things are working better than ever in a relationship. You can enjoy your everyday activities, especially such things as crafts or dressmaking. You can create some beautiful things.

Sunday the 11th. If you are feeling a bit ill, you will be wise to seek some advice about it from a knowledgeable friend. You may find a group of people a little boring. This can be a day for taking yourself off some-where alone. You will feel more hermitlike than usual. The day will be good for spiritual disciplines such as yoga. But take care not to overdo it or strain anything.

Monday the 12th. You will need to watch your health at present. This can be a time when you may feel quite low. Seeing a child in a hospital can make you feel depressed. You just may not be in the mood for all your usual activities. An escapist tendency can take you off somewhere for the day. Be careful how you treat co-workers lest you upset someone.

Tuesday the 13th. Things can seem to be quite changed for the better. You may feel much more like yourself and ready for fun again. However, you will need to watch an impulsive mood at times. You may rouse up a lot of rebellion in others if you try to be too con-trolling. Try to see another person's point of view. You may feel like a break from dealing with the public.

Wednesday the 14th. Your more sober and realistic ap-proach can work wonders. You may be angry about a partner's impulsive attitudes. However, you will be able to prevent a full-scale row from developing. An older friend will have some good advice to give you, but you don't seem prepared to listen. A group meet-ing can be noisy and quite irritating.

Weekly Summary

Social activities this week can be quite formal and even a bit staid. You will be more connected with older folks, especially in group matters. This can be more entertaining and far less serious than expected. Your partner's jolly and expansive attitude will make your outings very pleasant. Meeting an old friend may mean a lot of time spent gossiping and catching up on news.

You may be more inclined to retire and enjoy your

own company over the weekend. This can partly be due to the fact that you do not feel too well. Or you may have to care for someone else who is sick or in the hospital. Older people in a hospital or home are sure to be glad of your concern and interest. Sunday and Monday can be a bit of a struggle, but nothing lasts forever.

There can be a real shift in your attitude at the end of the week. Personal plans and concerns will be far more important to you. However, you need to watch a tendency to impose your will and desires on others. There is no doubt that you will start a minor rebellion if you do so. So try to balance impulse with reason. Be more realistic in your personal aims.

3rd Week/January 15–21

Thursday the 15th. You can go ahead with a property agreement. This can be a good time to go looking for a new car or other mode of transport. Computers or telephones may also be on your shopping list. You can, in fact, be interested in taking a course in order to develop new technological skills. Some of you may want to enroll for driving lessons.

Friday the 16th. This will be a good day for making money if you are a salesperson. You will enjoy buying clothes or attractive articles for everyday use. Buying a pretty present for a sick child can do a lot of good and help cheer up someone special. You are likely to be in a loving mood and ready to serve others with care. Business deals can be quite lucrative.

Saturday the 17th. This can prove to be a bonanza day for business matters if you are at work. You can clinch a deal with someone influential. It may be something you have been working on daily for a while. It will be a good day for enjoying your usual activities and routines both at home and at work. Co-workers can be very good company. A real sense of satisfaction can come from a job well done.

Sunday the 18th. You and a neighbor can have a very enjoyable day out together. You may be in the mood for some deep and serious pleasures. Some of you can tend to be fascinated with the occult or psychology just now. You may get a lot of books to read about these subjects. It may not be easy to talk about certain things with a partner.

Monday the 19th. You may feel as if you got out of the wrong side of the bed this morning. You really can feel stiff and tired. A journey can be most frustrating and full of delays and setbacks. Be prepared for long waits in traffic or at train stations. It's true; you do seem to have an air of resignation. Don't get too sorry for yourself though.

Tuesday the 20th. This can be a very lively time. The morning may see you and you mate dashing about busily trying to get shopping and various other errands done. A call from someone abroad will be very exciting. You may fall out with a lawyer or counselor later in the day. But keep an open mind to what is said. Be as tolerant as you can with other people's egotistical attitudes.

Wednesday the 21st. In many ways, this can be an odd and surprising time. A partner may be inclined to disagree with some of your plans. At work, it can be hard to get your message across to employees. A machine may let you down when you least expect it. This can be very irritating. You will feel tense and anxious. This may be due to family problems.

Weekly Summary

Your personal finances will need some attention and thought this week. You seem to have a lot of plans and ideas on how to make a bit more cash. This may mean having to improve the daily running of a business so that it can be more profitable. If you have to take a course in computers or to learn to drive, you can plan toward this in your budget. It can be a very good time for property matters. You may find the home of your dreams this week.

A lot has to be dealt with over the weekend. This may simply mean a lot of shopping in your local area. You and a mate can be kept busy with errands and lots of little journeys to sort things out. This will not be an easy time for travelers over long or short distances. Try to avoid Monday morning unless you really have to be on the road. A neighbor can be very amusing and pleasant company. News from abroad is sure to be stimulating.

The end of this period can see some unexpected events occurring at home. This will tend to throw you a bit and make you feel quite jittery. A family member is not being too cooperative about certain plans. You will have to explain the details more thoroughly and hope to convince everyone.

4th Week/January 22–28

Thursday the 22nd. Although you can be in a very loving mood toward the family, a mate or spouse may tend to feel very angry about something. You can conclude a very creative enterprise with a partner. The day will be good for property deals. You may be very busy settling down into a new and spacious home now. There will be a lot to do to get things straight and as you like them.

Friday the 23rd. Directing your talents in the right way can mean a sense of achievement. You will feel really powerful and dramatic. This can be ideal if you are an actor or connected with the theater in some way. Don't take the critics too much to heart, whatever your creative flair. You can tend to worry a lot about certain details that aren't quite right. But nothing is ever perfect.

Saturday the 24th. You can spend this day quietly working on your favorite hobbies or creative projects. Children will be more easygoing than usual. Little of great interest is likely to occur. You can just be glad to be alive. Get on with the things you enjoy, that make you feel good about yourself. Theatrical people may find this a quiet night for giving a performance.

Sunday the 25th. You ought to be a lot more enthusiastic and busy now. Spiritual matters are likely to be of importance to many of you. You can perform any duties needed with energy and interest. If you are in the mood to give the kitchen a good cleaning, this will be the time for it. You may need to have a detailed discussion with others about family finances.

Monday the 26th. Those of you who are learning a particular craft can have quite a hard time. You may get very frustrated when things just will not go right. Maybe you are being too hard on yourself or taking other people's criticisms too much to heart. A more philosophical attitude will help when dealing with a sick relative. You will feel somewhat imprisoned by boring everyday events.

Tuesday the 27th. If you are involved in medicine and healing activities, this can be a good day for such things. Your compassionate attitude can help others a good deal. You seem to be very powerful and can really shine at whatever you do. Crafts and cooking will go well and you can really enjoy playing the host tonight. It will be a good day for buying clothing or cars.

Wednesday the 28th. You and a partner can make a very good team now. You will need to start early on a journey if you want to avoid delays. The day will be good for getting engaged or married. You will feel ready to make a new start in a relationship. A more serious approach to a legal matter will ensure that nothing is overlooked. You are sure to do well in court.

Weekly Summary

This is likely to be a good week for creative interests and occupations. You Leo people love to be creating and feel at your happiest when you can be left in peace to get on with it. Those of you who like writing may get a bit frustrated when things don't come out as you would like. You seem to be easy prey to negative criticism this week. Have faith in your own abilities. Children can be very demanding at times.

You may have a lot of routine tasks and activities to deal with this weekend. Those of you who are involved in religious programs can be kept busy getting things organized. You may find that dealing with too many things at once can be a bit tiring on Monday. However, you will be determined to be calm and dutiful. Take care of your own health during this time. You may find that you have a lot of sick people to take care of.

This can be a good week for those who are ready to embark on an engagement or marriage. You seem ready to begin afresh, even in a long-standing relationship. Those of you who are involved in legal matters, professionally or otherwise, will find things going your way this week.

5th Week/January 29–February 4

Thursday the 29th. You will be in a most expansive and good-humored mood this morning. A dear partner can make you feel happy and contented. You may feel that above all you are good friends. Later on, you may have to deal with a variety of corporate and joint money matters. You may feel quite annoyed about something but ready to let the feeling pass.

Friday the 30th. This is sure to be a good day for making some extra cash. You can really get things organized and working the way you want them. Relationships with fellow workers will be harmonious. Those of you dealing with payroll accounts will find things flowing well and the job much easier than usual. Cooking or crafts may take much of your time.

Saturday the 31st. Contracts and agreements will work out well. You can find that a car or other piece of machinery you purchase will make your daily activities much easier. A loved one is ready to shower you with charming gifts or flowers; you can enjoy talking sweet nothings together. A brother or sister is likely to be in an astonishingly charming and lovable mood.

Sunday February 1st. You may have made plans for a journey some time ago, maybe even packed your bags. You can wave goodbye to dishes in the sink and other everyday things for a bit and enjoy yourself. A spiritual adviser may want to see you about some arrangements. If you are a teacher or a student, you may be feeling regretful if this is your last day of freedom.

Monday the 2nd. You are likely to be very cheerful and happy. This can be a good morning for you to see a lawyer or a counselor. A mate or spouse can be very generous and giving. You can enjoy traveling or just learning things together. The afternoon will be a slightly anxious time at work. A mislaid message or file can cause quite a bit of a panic.

Tuesday the 3rd. You can find this a tense day at work. You may find that a boss wants to implement some change. But you will be most unwilling to go ahead with the idea. As far as work is concerned, you do like things to keep to a steady pattern. A partner can be very awkward and annoying. Try to be patient if you can. Children may tend to be rebellious.

Wednesday the 4th. A careless or intolerant attitude can lead to some problems professionally. You Leo actors will do well as long as you don't get too carried away with yourselves and upset those who can help you. Trying to get through various routine activities can be a nightmare at times. You may get a bit temperamental if things don't work out the way you plan.

Weekly Summary

The start of the week may find you very much involved in various schemes and plans to make some extra cash. This can be through crafts, dressmaking, cooking or teaching others various skills. Whatever you can earn is likely to be put into a joint endeavor or family plan. You will be quite idealistic about all you do just now. Some of you may be quite involved in raising funds for charitable purposes.

A very good week can be had by those who are traveling. You may be having a wonderful time overseas in some relaxing atmosphere, maybe even honeymooning. Or you may be nearer home, just getting in a break before the hard work begins. You can open up your mind to new scenes and places. Even if you have to travel for work purposes, you are likely to take your partner with you and have pleasant company.

It can be a bit of a trial for those in the public eye at the end of this period. You may clash with other prominent people over matters of principle. Don't be too insensitive to the needs of others you are working with. Things can be successful if you keep calm and use your imagination.

6th Week/February 5–11

Thursday the 5th. In some ways a social event tonight can subtly change your life. You may find that a political group of people are not as committed as you are to ideals. You will meet some interesting and way-out folks. You need to be a little less serious and dictatorial about your philosophies. Students can be finding a course tougher than they thought.

Friday the 6th. Although you may be in the mood to go out, there seems to be little happening on the social scene. You can enjoy just meeting a good friend and indulging in a little gossip. At present you will be thinking a lot about your future goals and wishes. However, these may still be at the planning stage. Group activities will be highlighted.

Saturday the 7th. Although you will feel quite active and wide-awake, you are likely to keep yourself to yourself. This can be a good day for engaging in spiritual activities such as meditation, contemplation, and so on. You may be interested in studying depth psychology. Or you may enjoy just curling up with a good crime story or a film on TV.

Sunday the 8th. You may feel very rejected by a loved one just now. It may simply be due to a clash of ideas and aims. You seem to be changing your mind about someone quite often. However, try not to be so serious about it all. Spiritual matters just don't meet up with your expectations at present. Others may just be too materialistic or preachy for your liking.

Monday the 9th. You will be a bit disillusioned with someone. You really need to be more realistic in your approach to a partner. No one is perfect all the time. You can be trying to deceive someone. This is risky, and you may come a cropper. Some of you may be feeling anxious if a loved one seems to be undergoing some strain at present.

Tuesday the 10th. If a mate or spouse is sunk in a moody silence, you will be wise to try and cheer them out of it. It is useless just to get depressed or steam with suppressed anger. You need to take care not to strain yourself if you are lifting heavy machinery. Some of you may have to take personal responsibility for elderly relatives.

Wednesday the 11th. Maybe things can come to a head on this night of the Full Moon. You really need to confront someone who has been nagging you of late. Why put up with bad feelings when they may turn out to be just a lot of nonsense after all? The time is not so good for legal matters. An influential person seems to have made a mess of things. You may feel that no one is to be trusted.

Weekly Summary

This cannot really be counted as one of your best weeks so far. You are likely to find that your social life is so annoying that you would rather be alone, thank you. A particular group of people whom you hoped would support you in some issue seem to fall short of your expectations. Be cautious about getting involved in some political issue. You may stir up the authorities in some way.

Keeping yourself to yourself will be the best thing to do over the weekend. You may be involved in various spiritual matters. These can improve your state of mind for a little while. But you do seem to be a bit fed up with life. Visiting elderly people can seem to be a drag and a duty. However, you will be determined to do your bit. You will need to watch a tendency to hector or bully others into your way of seeing things.

After the weekend, you and a mate or a business partner can be headed for a real showdown. You Leo people do tend to make a drama of things at times. However, this can be the best way to clear the air of any mistrust, doubt, or bad feeling. If you are involved in a legal situation, be sure to take care of all the details. Don't be too trusting or gullible.

7th Week/February 12–18

Thursday the 12th. Taxes and other money matters seem to be causing a few headaches. You can get your message across to a partner calmly and quietly. The day will be good for dealing with salespeople and the public's needs. You may need some new machinery or a new car to help out with your job. Children seem to be require new uniforms and other school supplies. This can be expensive.

Friday the 13th. No need to get alarmed by the date; this will turn out to be a very pleasant day. You should certainly do well with any personal financial deals. Investments in food, clothing, or medical supplies are all likely to do well now. You may be interested in flower remedies, color therapy, or other alternative cures. Shopping can be fun.

Saturday the 14th. It can be a very creative Valentine's Day for students or teachers. You romantics may enjoy a little journey to some seaside resort with a partner. Research work can involve a neighbor, who may have some interesting information for you. You are likely to enjoy working with children who need special care and attention. The day will be good for travel, especially short local journeys.

Sunday the 15th. This is likely to prove a frustrating day for for those who have to go to work or make other local journeys. There can be delays and other problems on the roads and trains. You may find yourself out on a limb over a matter of principle. An elderly neighbor may be in trouble and need some help. You will tend to feel a little depressed about something.

Monday the 16th. This can be a good time for a meeting with a brother or sister. An older person will have a lot to tell you this morning. You will be more relaxed and at ease with others. This certainly can help communications between you. A family matter may puzzle you later on. You can feel a bit anxious about someone who is feeling ill.

Tuesday the 17th. An unexpected event may upset your domestic arrangements. You may find that a mate or spouse is acting a bit oddly. Perhaps you both are in need of a change. Maybe you have become too housebound of late. A gathering of relatives can take place in your home, but you will not enjoy it very much and may feel oddly detached.

Wednesday the 18th. Now things will liven up for you. A dinner party or other entertainment at home will go very well. You can feel much happier and more cheerful. A lot of money may be spent refurbishing a shop or the home and garden. However, it will be well worth it in terms of value. You are more likely to enjoy your daily activities now that you feel more energetic.

Weekly Summary

You can put a lot of time and thought into improving your personal bank balance this week. This may mean having to juggle certain stock investments and sort out taxes and insurance. On the whole, things look good; recently you seem to have made some wise investments in gilt-edge and secure places. You should be getting quite a steady income from some source. However, it may mean keeping hard at work on it every day.

Dealing with neighborhood matters will be time-consuming. You may be taking an interest in a child's education. This can mean having meetings with teachers, chats with local people to find the best schools, and so on. It will be a good time for any shopping expeditions in your local area. However, Sunday will not be a good time to go traveling. You will be wiser to sit in your armchair and look at vacation brochures instead.

This can be a time for entertaining your family and friends at your place. You will seem to be in a bit of a tizzy about it all on Tuesday. You may just be tired of the same environment and need a change. This can mean hunting an apartment for some of you. You may need to break away from parental restrictions and demands.

8th Week/February 19–25

Thursday the 19th. It seems that you are determined to have a good time. A partner can be very gentle and tender. You are more likely to have a sensitive approach toward a lover or a child. Those of you who are in therapy can find a doctor most sympathetic and easy to talk to in depth. You may feel quite rich and need some advice on handling your finances.

Friday the 20th. A trip late tonight to see an elderly in-law can be very enjoyable. You will feel quite virtuous about doing your duty. Going to the theater will reflect your taste, which is leaning toward serious entertainment of late. You may feel angry about a bungled financial matter. However, you will be able to keep your temper under control and prevent a scene.

Saturday the 21st. This will be a good day for dealing with routine activities. If you are having some health problems, you may be wise to see a consultant or other specialist in your ailment. You can find that a talk with a therapist or counselor is very good for you. Higher-ups if you are at work can be in real rapport with staff. Salespeople can do particularly well.

Sunday the 22nd. Seeing to an older person's daily needs can be a bit of a burden at times. You may feel a bit stiff and find it hard to get going. Take care not to overdo a job you are involved in, as you can strain yourself. You are eager to have some deep and philosophical conversations with special individuals. Perhaps you hope they will have a few answers.

Monday the 23rd. You will seem quite happy and contented dealing with your daily activities and tasks. Trade will be brisk for shopkeepers and stallholders this morning. You will want to make your workplace attractive and may set about decorating or improving it in some way. Later in the day, a meeting with an influential public figure can be most enlightening and inspiring.

Tuesday the 24th. Things can really change between you and a partner now. You can use your magnetic influence and charm to get things going the way you want. Try not to be too manipulative if you don't want a downright rebellion on your hands. You tend to speak out of turn and say things you will later regret. Be more cagey, especially about a money matter.

Wednesday the 25th. Things can be quite amicable and detached between you and a mate just now. You are not in the mood to stir up anything. In fact, you may prefer to be together with a group of friends rather than alone. Those working with the public will have a quiet day, with little happening. This will be a far better time to go out buying goods rather than selling them.

Weekly Summary

This will be a good time to get out and about and have some fun. You will have a real desire to live it up. A partner or a lover will seem game to fall in with all your plans. You seem to have very serious interests these days. Many of you can be trying to get somewhere with a creative project or a special hobby. Sports activities also are likely to be high on your list of fun things to do this week.

It can be a bit of a bore having to get back to the daily grind after such a lovely couple of days. However, duty calls and back you must go. You may come across some problems at work. Possibly an official inquiry is causing some holdups. You need to be patient if you can. Those of you in charge of an office or business should now establish a good rapport with your staff; this can help the turnover considerably.

Dealing with other people is not all that easy for you Leos. You tend to want your own way most of the time. Naturally, this can arouse some antagonism and opposition from partners or friends. Take care what you say to your nearest and dearest on Tuesday.

9th Week/February 26–March 4

Thursday the 26th. This can be a good time to make a fresh start with your finances. You can ask for some advice about an investment from an accountant or other experienced person. Your hopes for a creative matter seem to come to nothing, which can be quite upsetting. You tend to be too controlling when it comes to a corporate money matter. Allow others their say as well.

Friday the 27th. You will do really well on a property deal. You may be putting your all into some joint financial matter. It seems important for you to be working in attractive surroundings these days. You may get down to redecorating the home or shop. You will feel very contented just being busy about the place and dealing with everyday events.

Saturday the 28th. A trip to the coast can be really therapeutic for you and a partner. You will enjoy yourself in unusual ways and unusual places. Breaking out of your routine can do you all good. An air journey can be exciting. Students will get on well with their research and writing. Some of you may find a spiritual conversion taking place.

Sunday March 1st. You can have some troubles while traveling today. A hypocritical approach to someone will not help a lot. You need to be open and honest about the things you believe in. A philosophical matter may need to be shared with a loved one. You tend to be realistic about life. Just getting on with your daily affairs can take priority over flights of fancy.

Monday the 2nd. Things will go very well for you professionally. You can really make your mark, especially in some legal matter. This will be a good day for being expansive and in control of things. A boss will have some good words to put in about you, which may lead to promotion. A partner may come up with some unusual ideas to help your career. You should be confident and happy.

Tuesday the 3rd. A meeting at work can be most instructive. You will enjoy good conversations when out socially tonight. A brother or sister may have some ideas for a family money-making venture. Contracts can be signed and an agreement made on a business matter. Writers will do well and add to their professional skills.

Wednesday the 4th. You may try to do too much socially tonight. You and a partner can be in the mood for some different activities and enjoyments. A group meeting will go well enough, but you may feel that you have a lot of persuading to do on certain issues. You can be cheerful enough just being busy around the house. You may find it easier to accept that duty comes before pleasure just now.

Weekly Summary

It isn't always easy to think of new ways of getting a business going. However, with a little pushing and wheeling and dealing, you can get things moving this week. You tend to be a bit dictatorial at times, it's true, but nothing would ever get done if you didn't use your power and charm. You seem to know all the right people to approach when looking for a loan or contract. It will be a busy week but likely to be good financially.

You may have various schemes and dreams for a trip or vacation. Now can be the time to make these come true with a little persistence and effort. You may have to tear yourself away from your absorbing interests at work or home and take yourself off to see an in-law. Students can find that they are feeling a bit lazy and disinterested in their work.

Your professional life will seem to be going well. You seem to have made some friends in the right quarters, and they have a lot of good things to say about you. You will be very confident about some recent innovative ideas for a media concern. However, you will be wise to get others to work with you as a team instead of trying to go it alone.

10th Week/March 5–11

Thursday the 5th. You will be quite witty at a gathering. Jokes and puns can flow endlessly. A group you are involved with can be serious and philosophical types. You are likely to gain a lot of wisdom and understanding from these encounters. But you just may feel really bored as well. Young people may need organizing if they are having a party or other social function away from home.

Friday the 6th. There can be a lot going on right now that you are keeping from others. You may have some private deals up your sleeve. A property matter will need some careful consideration. Don't rush into any hasty decisions, no matter how good things look on the surface. Your sympathy and love for a mate or spouse can mean giving up something personal for the dear one's sake.

Saturday the 7th. Despite travel problems, you will be in a pretty confident mood. Enjoy being on your own and watching the world go by. A spiritual guide can be a bit too rigid and pedantic at times, and you will feel a bit weary of being preached at. An elderly in-law may be glad of your support and advice. Visiting others in a nursing home or hospital can make you feel wanted.

Sunday the 8th. There will be no stopping your exuberant personality from shining forth this day. You are likely to be in a chatty and cheerful mood. However, take care that you listen to a partner's needs or anxieties. You may be so full of yourself that you miss what is under your nose. You can be most sympathetic when you want. Some inspirational ideas can help students with their work.

Monday the 9th. Just enjoy yourself in your own way, and don't let opposition put you off. It can be a trying day for those dealing with taxes and insurance or legal matters. You may tend to feel that might makes right. You underestimate your own power and personal charisma at times. This can cause a bit of reaction and rebellion from a mate or spouse.

Tuesday the 10th. Some of you Leo people may find romance on the campus. You can feel quite stirred up by a lively debate with someone attractive and interesting. Sports activities can be great fun, although they may mean traveling some distance to participate in or view. You will be in the mood to do your own thing. Personal plans and interests are likely to be first and foremost.

Wednesday the 11th. You may have to contest a will or a tax matter. You can be acting a bit too heavy-handed over a corporate money matter. Maybe it would be wise to hold back a little. This will not be an easy day for those involved in banking, insurance, or other financial concerns. You may be careless or overoptimistic at times. Check everything over with care.

Weekly Summary

At the start of this period, you will want to get people together behind the scenes. You will be wise to shun the limelight when private deals and activities are to be discussed. This can be a time of important decisions for some of you. You will be wise to take time off alone and give it all deep thought. Do not make any hasty decisions. A retreat or a spiritual weekend can help get things in perspective again.

Your ever-ebullient personality will soon shine forth again. There's no keeping a Leo under a cloud. You are likely to enjoy interesting debates and discussions with others, especially if you can take a leading role. Some of you will attract a prospective lover with your wit and vivacity. Those already partnered can rekindle enthusiasm in your mate or spouse. But don't get too carried away with personal power. Otherwise you will produce the opposite reaction pretty swiftly.

After the weekend, take some time to sort out personal financial matters. You may need some advice if you think someone is overdoing the demands on taxes and other bills. You can get pretty stirred up about the whole thing.

11th Week/March 12–18

Thursday the 12th. This can be a pretty tough time all around. You can find that a boss or other influential person is at odds with you. Trying to get a corporate matter resolved may need all your powers of persuasion. A bank manager doesn't seem ready to play ball. However, you are ready to talk the hind leg off a donkey and mean to get your way.

Friday the 13th. Now put all the superstitions behind you about the date. It is sure to prove a lot easier and more flowing than you hoped. You will find this a very good time to have a chat with a business partner and sort out a few problems. Dealings with teachers and students will be successful. Young people can be great fun to work with. Traveling salespeople can do well.

Saturday the 14th. This is likely to turn out to be a busy, varied, and complex day. If you are traveling on business, things can get pretty lively at times. However, you can really enjoy some pleasant company on your travels. People can give you some unusual new perspectives and philosophies on life. Dealings made by letter, phone, or fax will be satisfactory.

Sunday the 15th. The morning may feel like a nonstarter. Everything will seem to conspire against you. Students can find it hard to get anything done. So many things will keep happening to frustrate your efforts. It may be sensible to stay at home and not try to make a journey unless you really have to. Delays and cancellations can make traveling a nightmare.

Monday the 16th. A family situation may develop and have to be sorted out. A partner seems to be in a muddle about something, or may be worrying needlessly. Try to be as sympathetic and sensitive as you can. You tend to have little patience with people who feel sorry for themselves. You need to be very straightforward about a money matter. Why keep it a secret?

Tuesday the 17th. This can be an upsetting day for family matters. Some of you will feel that things are changing very rapidly between yourself and a mate or spouse. A partner may be taking a break away from home for a while. Or perhaps you will want a change yourself. You are likely to be restless and irritable around the house. Why not get out for a visit?

Wednesday the 18th. You will be able to sort out a property matter with someone influential. A parent can be very helpful with a loan or other practical help. You can find that an older child needs some support and attention. Tune in to a partner's needs. You can enjoy a party or other unexpected get-together with a friend. A mate may surprise you with a gift.

Weekly Summary

A lot of running back and forth can make this a busy period for you. You may find yourself making lots of journeys around your local area and constantly bumping into neighbors you haven't seen for a while. This can be good fun; it can be great to catch up on local gossip. Although this can be a good time for traveling around, be careful on Sunday, as delays on roads and rail can make life a trial. Educational issues can be of burning interest this week.

Matters concerning your family will be a source of uneasiness these days. You may be going through a bad patch with a parent or mate. If you have been cooped up at home for too long, you are likely to begin pacing about like a caged lion. Those of you who are trying to sell property and make a move may find that others are not keeping their word. Keep your sense of humor and your faith, and all will turn out well in the end.

You and a loved one can certainly find ways to enjoy yourself. This may be a very good idea after all the ups and downs you experience this week. Going to the theater, especially on Wednesday, can mean that a surprise will be in store for you. Things can be quite romantic again by this time.

12th Week/March 19–25

Thursday the 19th. You may have some high hopes for the day, and you seem prepared to spend a bit to realize them too. A partner can have some bright ideas about spending the day together. You may be quite excited about some special event you are planning to attend or be involved in. The day will be good for team sports. On the whole, this will be a most enjoyable day.

Friday the 20th. Your pleasures now can be somewhat serious ones. You will find this a good time to get organized with hobbies and other creative projects, long pending. Students are likely to be very keen about their work but practical too. Your realistic attitude will be helpful to a child or a lover.

Saturday the 21st. Although you will be mainly involved with daily routine, you will feel relaxed and happy. A raise or bonus in a pay envelope will go a long way toward making you feel good. Co-workers will be cheerful and cooperative. This will make your work flow far more smoothly. You are likely to get a good deal done and feel on top of things.

Sunday the 22nd. This can be one of those days when, whatever you say, you get it wrong. You need to take care not to sprain yourself or take a fall this morning. Don't overdo household activities. You may be worried about a small pet. A partner's sensitive attitude can help you to get over a feeling of depression or poor health. Your teeth may trouble you.

Monday the 23rd. You and a business partner may have to see an accountant or bank official. A lawyer should be consulted about a will you and your spouse want to make. The day will be good for those undergoing counseling for their relationship. You can be very detached about things and see them far more clearly. A sense of power can help when dealing with the public.

Tuesday the 24th. Things appear to be loving and relaxed between you and a mate. You will both take a far more sensible attitude toward your relationship. Elderly in-laws can give the benefit of their wisdom. You will enjoy going to talks, lectures, and debates with others. You aren't likely to be in the mood to be alone just now, but need company and attention.

Wednesday the 25th. You may be inclined to have a good time, no matter what the cost. You can, in fact, be rather willful and demanding at times. Don't try to manipulate a lover emotionally; it can misfire on you. Feelings of jealousy and possessiveness from another may make you want to run a mile. Children can be pretty unpleasant at times.

Weekly Summary

This can be a time for getting down to some of those creative ideas that keep buzzing about in your head. You Leo people do love to be busy with lots of projects. At present you really want to share your talents and interests with others. A lover can be of great help in getting you inspired with hobbies or creative things. You may find that this is a constructive time. A lot can be achieved with a little discipline.

Although the weekend will be busy with various mundane and everyday activities, you can be very much at peace and contented. It may be rather a relief just to be ordinary at times. Your thoughts appear to be realistic, even serious. Worry about a small pet or someone's health may make Sunday morning somewhat stressful. Keep calm and deal with things one at a time. Take care not to overstrain yourself in your newfound enthusiasm for housework and other projects.

You and a spouse seem to be making real efforts to work out any differences of opinion. Some of you may be seeing therapists or counselors in order to get a third party opinion. This can be a good time for business partnerships too. However, you need to see that power is evenly distributed between you.

13th Week/March 26–April 1

Thursday the 26th. This can be a very lucky day for gamblers and speculators, wheelers and dealers. You will find that your faith in a certain financial project has been justified, as expected. Some of you will benefit from an inheritance now. This can give a sense of freedom and expansion to your life. The day will be good for those who have to buy for warehouses or other bulk needs.

Friday the 27th. If you play your cards right, you can get some quite important new business venture going. You seem to be lucky, and your gambles are paying off. Matters connected with shipping can do very well. You will be glad of a partner's intuitive insights and gut feelings. Don't ignore advice, however odd it may seem at times. You will feel in a confident and powerful position.

Saturday the 28th. This can be a very good time for those taking a vacation or going on a special journey. You and a loved one will feel very responsible for an elderly person's welfare. You may give talks and lectures on serious and philosophical subjects. You can be very calm and considerate of others. You can also expect the same treatment yourself.

Sunday the 29th. The morning may be spent dreaming and fantasizing instead of getting on with things. Be more sensitive to a partner's funny little whims and ways. You will be angry with someone who acts the martyr. You may be introduced to a guru figure who can change your life and your ideas. You can benefit from a powerful teacher's ideas.

Monday the 30th. This will be a happy day for those who are in love. You may be tempted to overdo the eating and drinking and making merry. But so what? It never hurts to have a mad day once in a while. You can be in a very generous and giving mood. Showering loved ones with gifts and taking them to splendid places will make you feel happy and loving. Professionally, this will be a most fortunate time.

Tuesday the 31st. This is likely to be a good time for raising funds for charitable events. You can find that a group of literary people will fire your imagination. It will be a good time also to get down to some creative work with others. You will enjoy a debate or discussion. Political meetings can really get you on your high horse. Write letters of complaint. You can put over your point forcefully and honestly.

Wednesday April 1st. You will enjoy a social function tonight despite its formality. Meetings and group activities can be practical and have a serious purpose. Working with groups of elderly folks or handicapped children can bring out the best in you. You may be more inclined to submerge your ego and work as a team with others. However, you still will be likely to have a leading role.

Weekly Summary

This week can be a very interesting one for you Leo students and teachers. Academic work of all sorts will appeal to you. You may be inclined toward philosophical or even spiritual interests. Photography and film can be rewarding pursuits financially as well as academically. You will be taking a large part in organizing and directing various things. A talk or debate is sure to be very lively and broaden your mind to many new things.

You may find that you are getting some new ideas and inspirations about a professional matter. But the ideas may still be unformed and a bit hazy. A business partner may be deceiving you in some way. It can be unintentional and worth giving the benefit of the doubt. However, you will be wise to tackle any peculiar situations as soon as they arise. You are in quite a powerful career position just now. So make the most of it.

The week will end on an interesting social note. Friends seem to be a lot older than yourself these days. Or you may be meeting with a group of people you haven't seen in a while. One way and another, interesting conversations, debates, and discussions will keep your mind fertile and alive.

14th Week/April 2–8

Thursday the 2nd. A quiet trip to see an art show can give you food for thought. You may enjoy some music in a private atmosphere. It will make you feel relaxed and peaceful. It can be important to keep a love affair under wraps just now. A more determined and serious approach to your studies can make sure that a lot gets done. You are more interested in spiritual disciplines.

Friday the 3rd. You may find that faith in something greater than yourself gives you a lot of joy. Reading spiritual or philosophical literature can be very rewarding. A journey you have to make for work purposes will prove successful. You may have to do some hard selling to put yourself across. Trying out a foreign language may present more problems than expected.

Saturday the 4th. It can be a good idea to put the brakes on now. You may not be feeling very well. A headache or stiff joints can hold you up from doing all you want. Be careful when working on dangerous tasks alone. You will need to exercise caution rather than foolhardiness. A journey can be frustrating and irritating. In-laws may wish to share some private problems.

Sunday the 5th. You can be very determined, even ruthless, with those who go against you. Personal plans and schemes may fly in the face of convention. But this will not put you off one jot. You will certainly meet with resistance from a mate or spouse if you get too bossy. Maybe you need to be a bit more detached, to see things from another person's viewpoint.

Monday the 6th. This ought to turn out to be a pretty successful day for purely personal interests. Your air of confidence will help a lot when dealing with teachers, students, or foreign people. You should find that leading a debate or discussion presents no problem. Your themes will tend to be serious as well as practical. Dealings with in-laws will be friendly.

Tuesday the 7th. It can be time for tax matters to rear their ugly head. You may be dismayed at what you have to pay out, especially if you are self-employed. You may try hard to control a particular deal, but things will not go quite the way you planned. Those of you in therapy or undergoing medical treatment may find this a tough day. But a great deal of pain can be released and understood.

Wednesday the 8th. This will be a far more relaxed day all around. You can enjoy going shopping, especially if you are abroad. But you may need to beware of too much extravagance just now. Finding a really good vacation offer can make you happy. A sense of freedom from a money worry will be a real relief to your system. You will be in a generous mood and ready to treat all who come your way.

Weekly Summary

This can be a time for sorting out a few private matters. Some of you may have become entangled in some secret relationship and now feel a bit worried about it all. You may, of course, have good reasons for keeping things out of the limelight, especially if you are a public figure. Others of you may be very much involved in spiritual or philosophical matters. You can find it difficult to keep up with the required spiritual disciplines at times.

You will be in a very determined and strong-minded mood over the weekend. Use your personality to push any private and personal plans through. But take care not to be too overbearing with anyone who disagrees with you or stands in your way. You do tend to play the dictator at times, even the quiet Leos. At your best, you may have a lot to teach others from your own past experiences. You will be especially in tune with young people.

Money matters will be a source of some annoyance this week. You may have to fill out tax returns or ask for a lot of insurance to be paid up for various reasons. However, this will not stop you from having a spending spree in a quite reckless manner on Wednesday.

15th Week/April 9–15

Thursday the 9th. It may be a good idea to use a quiet day like this to sort out your personal finances. Take a detailed look at what is going on, and you will feel a lot more in control. In many ways, you Leo people really enjoy keeping meticulous accounts and knowing where your money goes. Possessions generally can be evaluated now. Get rid of any unwanted clutter.

Friday the 10th. Journeys purely for pleasure can be special for you. You may find the language problem a barrier at times if abroad. But this will not stop you from getting where you want to go. Spend some time dealing with reforms and changes in educational matters. Local activities can be a bit disruptive when you are out shopping or visiting neighbors.

Saturday the 11th. Your self-possession may fail you a bit, as your mind can be on religious observances. You seem to feel that you have bungled something important. Or you may find yourself clashing with an authoritarian figure. An elderly in-law will be inclined to act in a rigid and defensive manner. Conservative viewpoints may be challenged. Be cautious if traveling in some strange foreign place.

Sunday the 12th. You can get really angry at a neighbor even on this religious holiday. The morning can be irritating if you are trying to get to church on time. Acting impulsively in traffic can get you in hot water. Later on, you can enlist a partner to help deal with some difficult youngster. A brother or sister may be creating a family problem that needs solving together.

Monday the 13th. In some ways, unexpected reactions from a partner can wake you up a bit. You seem to be using a lot of joint funds purely for your own pleasure and self-interest. An older neighbor can give you some very good advice or practical help. You will be quite calm and more detached than usual. Creative interests will entice you. However, you may be sporadic about them.

Tuesday the 14th. This will be an enjoyable though quiet sort of day. You can get on with various hobbies and interests without too much interruption. Children will be good-tempered and cheerful. They will not be likely to make a fuss or cause problems for you. A lover will be glad to be in your company. You can enjoy being at peace together.

Wednesday the 15th. A creative project may need someone to back it. Raising capital isn't too easy these days. However, you can be very charismatic and full of charm. Take care not to play the hypocrite, especially with a lover, who may demand the truth. You can have a confusing day at work. A recent decision will need to be made more clear.

Weekly Summary

This can be a very trying week for local activities and educational matters. You may feel let down by an authority figure, especially on Saturday. A school official or professor may be acting in a defensive and rigid manner. Or you can find that you just haven't been working hard enough at your studies. It will not be a good time for traveling around your neighborhood. There may be delays and traffic problems due to road construction.

A need for changes at home can get you into conflict with a mate. You will have quite different ideas about what you want done about the place. You may feel a need for more space and consider putting up an extension. Money can be another problem that you will need to discuss before going ahead with any new schemes and dreams. You tend to be impatient and impulsive with everyone.

All sorts of creative plans can be buzzing about merrily in your head right now. But the old worry of lack of necessary cash can really be a problem. This will not be a good time to take a gamble with anything. You must be sure that you make your situation clear first.

16th Week/April 16–22

Thursday the 16th. A quiet and disciplined approach to a child will be your best bet. You will need to sort out someone's carelessness over a money matter.

Things can improve between you and an elderly in-law.
You can enjoy yourself a good deal on a work trip. Let
your hair down a bit later in the day and relax. But be
sure you get your obligations sorted out first.

Friday the 17th. This can be a cheerful and energetic
day. Your pace will be more steady and even than
usual. A placid outlook can ensure that you and your
co-workers are on better terms. You will enjoy being
busy at work. A partner can be very helpful when a
decision has to be made. This will not be a day for
impulsive actions. You can be better able to deliberate
and be cautious and conventional.

Saturday the 18th. You can have a very happy day just
getting on with all life's busy little tasks and activities.
Love and good feeling will flow abundantly. Someone
can do you a real favor. You will be in a philanthropic
mood and may be eager to help others out. A beautiful
gift or a delightful tête-à-tête in private will make your
day complete.

Sunday the 19th. You may tend to disagree with the
views of a spiritual teacher or a professor. You can be
a bit restless with the everyday routine this morning
and fancy a change of some sort. A partner seems sympathetic with your needs. The afternoon can be spent
at the seashore or watching a good film together. Those
involved in photography work will be quite creative.

Monday the 20th. You will be able to take a different
approach to a partnership matter. Being detached
about a relationship can help a lot when discussing important issues. This will be a good day for teachers.
You may be able to give your subject a lot more power
and interest and can fascinate others. A group of people may share a creative interest or be involved in a
project with you.

Tuesday the 21st. A steady and sensible attitude toward a partner can be the best thing this morning. You will enjoy the company of an older person. A lot can be learned from someone's mature advice and experience. You will feel a lot more like your old self this afternoon. Confidence in your abilities will help when directing others at work. A boss may show gratitude by raising your salary.

Wednesday the 22nd. Those involved in accounting matters at work are likely to be very busy. Decisions may have to be made about a property or shipping matter. You may find a superior's motives hard to understand at times. Just play along with it all until you can see what is going on. This can be a very good time for making some capital and investing in a few things.

Weekly Summary

Daily rounds of activities seem to be pleasurable for you these days. You seem to be a much more easily pleased person than you used to be. In fact, just being ordinary can be a quite restful pursuit now and then. You can be quite busy making clothes, painting the kitchen, and so on. At work, you may find that you have to deal with accounts or other financial matters more than usual. Co-workers will be good-humored and jolly company.

A wish for someone interesting and different to talk to may get you involved with a group of unusual people this week. You may be introduced to someone powerful and dramatic. Your approach to others can be a lot calmer and more reliable now. This can be much appreciated by those who need some advice or support from you. Dealings with older people can be good.

Your confidence in financial matters can be very profitable this week. You can go ahead with a corporate scheme without too much worry. Others seem to trust your ability and judgment to make a good business deal. Use your intuition and you can really benefit financially this week. Joint funds can take a sudden leap for the better.

17th Week/April 23–39

Thursday the 23rd. With a little imagination, you can do very well with whatever you tackle. You may be more convinced by a partner's spiritual beliefs than before. The day will be good for studies in healing, photography, or mystical subjects. A trip to the shore can be very therapeutic for you and your mate. An air journey can be really fascinating.

Friday the 24th. A meeting can be very constructive. You will be able to deal successfully with new and unusual subjects in your studies. The day is likely to be particularly good for scientific matters or those dealing with astrology. You can enjoy a deep conversation with a brother or sister who shares your ideals and philosophies. Going to a meeting or seminar together can be fun.

Saturday the 25th. You will tend to be very serious about a study matter. Putting all else aside and getting on with revision or other work will be a wise move. Time seems to be running out fast. The afternoon may also mean getting on with work. But you will yearn to escape and can spend a good deal of time in a dream. This can be a good time for those buying rather than selling goods.

Sunday the 26th. Some of you will be considering a change in your professional careers. This can be a good time to sit down and work things out. A partner may be against your changing things; however, put your case over as best you can. Disruptions from others can mess up your day. You may get tense and irritable when various interests clash with one another.

Monday the 27th. You can make quite a lot of money through professional matters. Your charm and tact will stand you in good stead when dealing with public issues. A film tonight can be emotional and delightful. You are sure to enjoy being out and about on the town later in the evening. A spiritual group can give you a lot of insight.

Tuesday the 28th. A group can have a powerful effect upon you. You need to watch that someone isn't trying to manipulate your way of thinking, or that you in turn are not being too insistent on your own point of view. You can enjoy interesting company when out tonight. Good for going to the theater, especially if a thriller is on the program. Children may be inclined to be a bit mischievous.

Wednesday the 29th. Don't be too extravagant with your hard-earned cash. Use a little caution and common sense when arranging a social function or dinner party. You can be in for some unpleasant surprises at work. Partners may change their minds about some recent decision. You will be tense and irritable about a professional matter. However, you will manage to maintain an outward calm.

Weekly Summary

This will be a good week for Leo students. You will be quite inspired about some subject. You may feel that your experience in life is giving you a more spiritual approach to things. You will be able to share a lot of your feelings and ideals with a partner or other relative. Just talking about the things you believe in can help to make the world a better place. Books you read now can have a great influence on your thinking.

You may be involved in various new schemes and plans concerning your career. Generally, there is likely to be a desire to start afresh, which can lead to searching for a new job. Or you may just work out new and innovative ways of dealing with your present profession. There is no doubt that you are on to a good thing and earning lots of fees. Those involved with the public can certainly put themselves over well and are likely to gain from it.

This will be a good week for social activities. You may spend as fast as you earn on entertainment. Having friends to dinner can be costly, as you are always inclined to be too lavish. Exercise a little caution and practicality this time, and all will go well. Work may interfere with your social arrangements.

18th Week/April 30–May 6

Thursday the 30th. Certain private arrangements for tuition can work out very well. You may be able to do some work on the side to help promote career interests. Advertising and other forms of communication are good ways to get yourself known. You can keep yourself very busy at work and take an important role. But you are more likely to be the power behind the throne just now.

Friday May 1st. This is likely to turn out to be a very good day from a financial point of view. You can benefit from a work that has been published or some other private source of income. However, riches are not always material. You can feel very blessed in spiritual ways as well. Passing a test or exam can mean a lot to you, although it may mean little to others.

Saturday the 2nd. Things may get a bit confusing when dealing with a property matter. You need to sort out your own needs from those of a company just now. You can be inclined to be escapist and seek personal pleasures before anything else. This doesn't do anyone any harm now and then, so don't feel guilty. You may be a bit unrealistic about a financial speculation.

Sunday the 3rd. Others may accuse you of being too dictatorial and just a mite overbearing at times. You do seem to be aggressive when putting over your point of view. A boss may suddenly get in touch about a work matter. You can be restless and somewhat argumentative. Nor do you take kindly to a child's insubordination. Just try to be less stubborn with everyone.

Monday the 4th. If you can make an early start, you will feel the benefit of such a discipline. A great deal more can be achieved that is of real note. An older and mature person can give you some wise advice, so don't reject it. You will be seeing life and other people in a more sensible and realistic fashion now. In fact, you can be remarkably patient with slower people.

Tuesday the 5th. Your ability to take charge will stand you in good stead when dealing with the public. You can find a bank officer more sympathetic than usual about a loan or other backing you require. You can find that sorting out a mortgage problem is easier. This will be a good day for traveling to see beauty spots. The seashore can have a very beneficial effect and help you to relax.

Wednesday the 6th. If you have been too optimistic of late about a financial matter, you may have to look at things more carefully now. Certain careless mistakes can cost you dear. However, if all is going as planned, you may instead have cause to celebrate some good fortune. You may want to spend lavishly while away on a trip and count the cost later.

Weekly Summary

You seem to be acting on behalf of a boss in certain situations. This may mean keeping a low profile while also keeping things going. Private work should be paying well now. Some of you may be studying and preparing for examinations. This can mean a period of withdrawal from your usual social activities. You can get a lot done with a little bit of effort and discipline. An elderly relative in a home or hospital will be glad to see you.

You may be feeling guilty about taking some time off for a purely personal pleasure. Or you can go to extremes and give up your own needs entirely. There will not seem to be any halfway measure in your behavior. Take care not to alienate others on Sunday by some erratic or extreme behavior. You will need to watch your temper when in a public situation. You can figure prominently in a political matter that means a lot to you.

On the whole, this is a good time for your own finances to be sorted out and put into shape. You may have too many irons in the fire. This can become confusing and will spread your investments too thinly. Take time to take stock of what you now have going for you.

19th Week/May 7–13

Thursday the 7th. A love of beauty can inspire your studies. You may discover somewhere scenic and attractive near your own home. Being by the sea can be very inspiring for you now. You can really enjoy yourself on a vacation somewhere exotic. In fact, you are sure to be healed and transformed by whatever you encounter at present. A lover may be from a foreign place.

Friday the 8th. New acquaintances in your neighborhood will be very interesting. You can spend the day gossiping if a neighbor drops in unexpectedly. It will not be an easy time for team activities. You will be inclined to be tense and irritable, especially about a money matter. However, a certain amount of detachment will help when sorting out a tricky business deal.

Saturday the 9th. You can be bored with looking at the same old faces and places. You may have to help out an elderly neighbor this morning. If you feel a bit depressed, try to be philosophical rather than negative. Later on, you may feel a real urge to run away from everything. However, a loved one has the power and charm to talk you out of it.

Sunday the 10th. Your restless mood will continue. Home can seem very restricting to some of you. You will be wise to make a creative change such as redecorating or renovating rather than a huge upheaval. A partner may be tense and uncooperative. A friend whom you haven't seen for a while may come over to see you unexpectedly. You can be shocked at the change in the person.

Monday the 11th. You may be really annoyed about a family issue. A parent may be acting most unreasonably in your opinion. You need to be as good-humored as you can when dealing with joint money matters. In fact, you are likely to feel very generous toward someone. Beware of being too impulsive. An extension to the home can get under way. The evening will be good for going to the theater if you like action-packed plays.

Tuesday the 12th. If you have the will to get through a real work load, you are sure to find the way. This is likely to be a very busy day for you at work. However, it also is sure to be a profitable one. Those of you dealing with the public, especially when dealing with financial matters, can have a humorous and pleasant day. A lover will be warm and passionate.

Wednesday the 13th. You can have a very happy time with a loved one. You can both be in the mood to spend lavishly and enjoy yourselves. Outings with children can be fun. Money will really seem to be no object. There can be a good deal of fun and laughter to share. You seem to be in a highly creative mood right now. What you produce can be a regular little money-maker as well.

Weekly Summary

Take some care when driving about locally this week. You can run up against restrictions, fines, or other annoying official activities. You will be in the mood to keep moving about, and a lot of this cannot be helped. A partner may want you to come along on various trips to see neighbors. You will be keen to visit beauty spots or go to a museum and other places of cultural interest. News from distant friends or in-laws can be very stimulating this week.

Home life will not be all that sweet this weekend. This can be due to a partner's cranky attitude toward everything. Or it can simply be that you feel very restless of late. You really may need some sort of change of environment, even just for a bit. Although a parental figure is acting in an impulsive, even irritating, manner, you will be able to keep your sense of humor and can laugh at it all.

You may feel that a lover is being very possessive and jealous at times. A serious talk will help clear the air. On the other hand, it can make you both feel a deeper sense of separation. Again you will need to keep your sense of proportion and humor before others begin to turn difficult, maybe even unpleasant.

20th Week/May 14–20

Thursday the 14th. Long-term association can make you feel secure and comfortable. You may have to discipline a youngster, but you can be firm without being rigid. A sudden meeting with a fascinating person will brighten your trip to work. This can flare up into a momentary attraction, but it probably will not last for very long. You will enjoy an unusual activity with a group of people.

Friday the 15th. Maybe you feel just a bit lazy and not inclined to do your daily tasks. You may find that you are developing a sore throat. You may be hardhearted toward a loved one's demands. But it can be doing him or her a service. Try taking things a little easier if you can. Money spent on medicine may be a waste. Be more choosy.

Saturday the 16th. In many ways you can enjoy this day. The atmosphere if you are at work will be very cheerful and lively. However, you will have to keep up the pace and get through quite a work load. Trying to dodge things will not be a good idea. You may get some confusing messages from a partner. What is more, you may not be prepared to believe a thing he or she is saying.

Sunday the 17th. Be prepared for some surprises from a partner. You may get taken out unexpectedly to the theater or some other interesting place. You can enjoy one another and be cheerful. A friend may try to maneuver you into helping out with some children's activities. You can feel unsure what to do and keep changing your mind.

Monday the 18th. You are sure to be glad when a mate or spouse acts in a supportive way. You may need this when facing an angry parent or a difficult child. Try to keep from boiling over when a boss get you down. Although there can be a lot of energy bubbling over in the office, it can hardly be called harmonious. You can be rushed off your feet by lots of demands.

Tuesday the 19th. You can find that tax demands and other important bills make a big drain on your joint account. This may mean less to spend on life's little pleasures. A lover's possessive attitude may be hard to handle at times. You will have to try to talk things through rather than react explosively or emotionally.

Wednesday the 20th. Things look a lot happier where financial matters are concerned. You may be in for a bonus or a lucky win of some sort. You are likely to be in a very generous and giving mood with those you love. Deals made with foreign firms or individuals will be successful. Your trust and optimism about someone will be well rewarded.

Weekly Summary

Daily routines have a habit of getting pretty tedious. You will not really be in the mood to do a lot at home or at work this weekend. Try to relax a little and stop fretting over unnecessary details. You can be very concerned with beauty just now. This may mean buying new clothes or making things for the home. However, your tastes and needs can be somewhat grand. Take care of your health, as you can be prone to overeating. You could develop a decidedly sweet tooth this week.

Your mate or spouse is likely to be a little demanding at times. But you can be cheerful enough about it and not even resentful on Sunday. However, things can change a lot by the next day. You may be ready to blow your top at someone, probably the boss. There are times when discretion is definitely the better part of valor. This is likely to be one of them.

You are sure to be in luck this week. Wins on pools, lotteries, or just a nice little tax rebate can really cheer you up. You are not the sort to hang on to your good fortune. A generous streak may mean you ask all to enjoy life with you at the local bar. A business deal will go well on Tuesday.

21st Week/May 21–27

Thursday the 21st. A group of friends may go with you on a trip abroad. This can be enjoyable, especially if you are to study art, film, or music. You can feel spiritually refreshed and regenerated by the experience. Teaching others can be uplifting. You may take an interest in a child's creative activities. This will be a day for real enjoyment; you can broaden your horizons in more ways than one.

Friday the 22nd. A wonderful day can be spent looking at art objects, attending concerts, or simply lazing in the sun. You will feel relaxed and yet open to all sorts of new impressions about beauty. A partner can astonish you by voicing opinions that seem out of character. You may tend to be abrupt with someone and regret it later.

Saturday the 23rd. In some ways this can be a chaotic day for you professionally. You may feel guilty and anxious about certain matters left undone. However, your sense of sympathy will be helpful when dealing with a friend or a group of people. A partner can prove to be very insightful about a matter that has been nagging you. You may feel quite telepathic with a loved one.

Sunday the 24th. A phone call can soon settle a financial matter. You will enjoy having a spree in a mall or other Sunday market. Conversations with others are likely to be philosophical and deep. You can have a good deal of fun as well. Those appearing in public, such as actors and media personalities, will be most successful.

Monday the 25th. A new group of people you become involved with on this holiday may have active spiritual interests. Your may want to take some part in helping out with a charity matter. All sorts of idealistic intentions and feelings may abound. You can meet someone at a social function who feels like a soul mate. A lively evening can be spent in debate over political matters.

Tuesday the 26th. Don't be too trusting of newfound friendships. You need to be realistic about any money demands a group of people may make on you. You may confide too much in a particular friend and regret it. This can be a good time for active participation in charitable fund-raising activities. A partner can enjoy going to a romantic film with you tonight.

Wednesday the 27th. In many ways, a formal function tonight can be a bit boring. But you can find that meeting old friends is quite an experience. You tend to be quite forceful in expressing your ideas to others. Try to be a bit less dramatic. A group leader who is too demanding can make you feel very resentful. You can encounter opposition and have ego clashes with someone influential.

Weekly Summary

This can be a splendid week for anyone going on a special trip abroad. You seem likely to be bent on a cultural exploration of various beautiful places. You may be part of a group or even leading one for this venture. One way or another, there will be a sense of comradeship and sharing of your experiences with others. You can feel quite changed by all you see and do. Those involved in various studies and research work will do very well.

Your professional life may be undergoing some sort of reshuffle or even a period of disillusionment. You may wonder whether you are really living up to your own ideals and standards. An influential friend can help to cheer you up and reassert your usual self-esteem. You may have to sort out a few muddles or confusions that arise over a money matter. If all is aboveboard, you have nothing to worry about.

Socially, this will be a very good time. You can enjoy various group activities that may vary from spiritual sessions to political debates. You need to be detached and philosophical at times. Other people may be fixed in their ways, and you Leo people are not noted for your own flexibility either.

22nd Week/May 28–June 3

Thursday the 28th. If you feel a bit withdrawn, don't worry about it. Maybe it will be a good idea to take a break from your usual round of activities and spend a little time alone to contemplate. You will enjoy reading serious books, listening to classical music, having philosophical chats with a loved one. You tend to be serious in your outlook.

Friday the 29th. This will not be a good morning for travel. You can experience delays and irritations. A loved one may be quite unresponsive. This can make you feel sad and a bit depressed. But things are sure to change in no time. Your optimism about a piece of writing will be justified. You may see some cash returns for a really good professional idea. You may feel a bit tired and low.

Saturday the 30th. You are sure to be your old self now and ready for some action. If a partner acts passively, you will be in a challenging mood. Doing things that are different together may fly in the face of convention. But you really will not seem to care. A friend may annoy you at times. You may take over the leadership of a particular group of people.

Sunday the 31st. You have a far more sensible approach to things. This can help when dealing with an old in-law problem. You may be severe with a student. But it will be necessary to exercise some discipline. Be sure that you are not deceiving someone, however, unintentionally. You may find that a message is misunderstood or not even received.

Monday June 1st. Financial matters can be of importance now. You need to be on the ball, for you can face some challenges from others. In fact, this can be a day when your fighting spirit will rise in you. Your powerful position in a group may be threatened. A lover may be acting very emotionally and unreasonably. This can make you see red.

Tuesday the 2nd. You will need to exercise a little caution in a particular money matter. Your tendency is to be too trusting, maybe even gullible. Just keep an eye on what is going on before committing yourself. People seem to be trying to ram their political opinions down your throat. You naturally react to this with some resentment. Things can get a bit explosive at a group meeting tonight.

Wednesday the 3rd. Your attitude toward a neighbor is likely to be very helpful and sympathetic. You should be in very good form and a power to contend with. If you are in the mood to make some reforms in local matters, you may have to go canvassing for support. A partner seems to be on your side in all you want to achieve. This will be a good time for fascinating social activities.

Weekly Summary

You may be inclined to separate yourself from other people at the start of this period. This can be due to a serious outlook on life. Or you may just feel alienated or lonely at this point. It can be a good idea to reflect and be more introverted for a while. You may have to make a journey to see some elderly person in a home or hospital. This can be dutiful but also depressing.

You may feel quite worried about someone, or sad if they are not themselves. Your personal desire is to be of help to others and generous with time and money. Maybe some of these ideas and ideals, which are so personal to you, can be made real. But you do need to be cautious and not be taken in by every sob story you hear. A partner is likely to be a real support to you now. He or she can give you some practical advice and help.

Dealing with wills, taxes, and insurance matters can make you quite irritable at times. But you will need to buckle down to sorting out your personal finances. Don't be too trusting when dealing with a property matter. Not everyone is as open and straightforward as you are.

23rd Week/June 4–10

Thursday the 4th. You can achieve a great deal in your local area if you work with others as a team. In this way people are likely to take notice of what you have to say about education, housing, and other topics of interest. Increased communication with brothers and sisters can help to sort out some emotional problem among you. You actually will seem to enjoy a heated debate tonight.

Friday the 5th. You can feel very frustrated by a piece of news you hear sometime during the day. It will not be a very good time to go on a local shopping spree. Traffic and other delays can make you irritable. Be careful when driving, as you or others will be prone to impulsive actions. You will enjoy a group discussion later on. A more honest attitude with a sibling can help in understanding each other.

Saturday the 6th. Your professional interests may clash with family needs. This can create a lot of tension all around. You may have to use a lot of tact and charm to soothe ruffled feelings. A partner can be very down in the mouth. Single Leo people can meet someone excitingly romantic through their work. But it is likely to be a brief encounter, so don't pin any hopes on it.

Sunday the 7th. This can be a good day to be at home and enjoy the peace and quiet. You may have a friend drop in unexpectedly. But a little gossip and light-hearted banter can be good for you just now. A mate or spouse may be eager to take you on a little trip and then an evening out somewhere. However, you may feel more like just relaxing in the armchair with a favorite book or TV program.

Monday the 8th. You can be determined to do things the way you like them to be done. In fact, you may be a bit ruthless at times with a lover. A partner can be very sensitive to an emotional problem of yours. It will be a good day for creative activities. You may feel a sense of compulsion to get a project finished and off your chest. Children can be good company.

Tuesday the 9th. A surprise social affair can be double-edged. You may bump into someone you had rather not meet. Don't be too impatient when others disagree with you at a meeting. You need to be detached and keep an open mind if possible. Partners may tend to blow hot and cold in their affections. You can wonder just what is going on.

Wednesday the 10th. Those of you who are involved in some sort of gamble or speculation may find that you have counted your chickens before they have hatched. You can feel a lack of faith in some creative venture of yours. Maybe you would be wise to ask the advice of someone who is not involved. Later you will have to get down to the nitty-gritty of life and catch up on daily tasks.

Weekly Summary

This can be a week for campaigning for those of you who are involved in local political issues. You can have some unusual dealings with people in the neighborhood. A special local friend may invite you around for a talk or discussion. This can be a good time to get yourself down to the boring task of answering calls and letters that have mounted up. Be careful when traveling about on short journeys. You may be under tension, and this can cause accidents.

Family activities seem to be at odds with your need to get on with your career. But don't let a partner get into a mood. You will just have to compromise in some way. Have a good talk about it all, and maybe you can get the family to see your point of view. Or promise to take them all out to something exciting later on. A party you have in your home may not be an unmitigated success.

This can be a creative time for some of you Leo people. You are sure to want to have a little fun and enjoyment after all your recent hard work. This can mean going to the theater or just relaxing with a lover. However, things will not work out quite as you planned and schemed.

24th Week/June 11–17

Thursday the 11th. This should be a relaxed and peaceful day. You can get on quietly with work schedules and routine jobs. In fact, an air of contentment can make your company very pleasant for those you work with. You can shine at a talk or debate you attend tonight. Others are likely to be interested in what you say. Teachers or lecturers can accomplish much.

Friday the 12th. This will be another happy and cheerful day whether at home in the kitchen or busy at work. You can find that a good-humored attitude definitely pays off. You are likely to feel generous to co-workers or employees. Raising their wages or otherwise rewarding their efforts is sure to make you very popular. You can really enjoy a pet's company.

Saturday the 13th. This can be a good time to be with loved ones. You tend to be cheerful, though a bit possessive, just now. A mate or spouse will be glad of your attention and sensitive care if he or she is not well. You may feel a bit under stress over some financial matter. However, if you play your cards right and use your intuition, you can end up doing well.

Sunday the 14th. This will be a good time for you and a mate to get out and about and enjoy yourselves. You can find a public place distasteful and ugly. Perhaps the service in a restaurant will be particularly bad. You are likely to speak up, but try to be as tactful as you can. You may find a doctor's advice helpful when dealing with a partner's ailments.

Monday the 15th. If you keep working away, doing overtime and pushing yourself so hard at work, you will begin to feel under the weather. A child may need to be reprimanded for some naughtiness. You can find that a lover's possessive or jealous attitude makes you feel cold and disinterested. You can enjoy philosophical discussions with a group of people tonight.

Tuesday the 16th. You may be too impulsive over a money matter. This can be a time of busy social activity. You can feel as if there isn't time to breathe. A concert or art show tonight can be wonderful. It may be hard to resist spending a fortune on beautiful things.

You can feel very edgy with a loved one. A desire to change things can make you spoil for a fight.

Wednesday the 17th. You need to have some faith in a friend's advice. This afternoon, you may find that a private meeting or discussion with a legal adviser can help in a marital matter. You may be very much bothered about a financial deal. This can involve an inheritance. It seems that your wish to expand a business may have to be kept on hold for a while.

Weekly Summary

Keep going with your daily activities, and a lot can be achieved. You can be quite relaxed and at peace at the start of this week. Relationships with co-workers and staff are likely to be most harmonious and pleasant. You can get a raise and feel very happy about it. Those of you who are involved with pets, especially dogs and horses, will enjoy being with your favorite friends this week. You can be less critical and more tolerant than usual.

A partner will be glad of your self-control and ability to cope in all circumstances. If your love has been unwell of late, you may be able to offer a lot of tender care. Legal matters can cost a lot, but you seem determined to get on with whatever you have started. You may have some interesting and revealing talks with a counselor. The need to be totally honest and open can really help with a marriage or other partnership problem.

After the weekend, you can find yourself very busy with joint financial matters. This may mean having to put in some extra work in order to pay off certain debts. Or you may need to start saving up for a special holiday. However, your shoulders seem broad enough to take on any fresh burdens.

25th Week/June 18–24

Thursday the 18th. A sudden break from the old routine can be really energizing for you. You may make a sudden decision about a relationship matter. If someone has been getting you down with changeable and explosive behavior, you may be better getting away for a while. An entertainment shared with in-laws can turn out to be more lively than expected.

Friday the 19th. A teacher or professor may be able to help you with a study problem. You will shine at a social luncheon or other occasion early in the day. A buildup of work may mean having to go in and tackle a muddled situation. A partner may be acting very oddly about a professional matter. You need to be more sensitive to someone's needs and not too rigid in your views.

Saturday the 20th. Using technology and other means of communication can enhance work output. You may be busy arranging a private little business deal. People just do not seem to be reacting the way you hoped they would. In fact, there are times when you may have to deal with some insubordination. You tend to overreact to other people's attitudes at times.

Sunday the 21st. This can be a favorable day for those in the public eye. You will find that your feelings change for the better. A more tolerant and good-humored attitude will help a lot when dealing with others. You may be inclined to spend a lot on food and entertainment activities; but if this is relaxing, go ahead. You may want to raise funds for a charity.

Monday the 22nd. It will be a good idea to get out for a while and have some social activity. You seem to be involved with some quite different and even eccentric people just now. You may be obliged to take some work home with you and deal with it where you can be alone and quiet. This will be a good day for those involved in bulk buying for warehouses and stores.

Tuesday the 23rd. Carelessness can cost you dear this morning. You will tend to be lavish while entertaining others. A social occasion may turn out to be a bit over-elaborate. You will find a theatrical production very dramatic. A boss may ask you to take charge of a new venture, which will mean a journey overseas or some distance away. A teacher can help you to be constructive with your studies.

Wednesday the 24th. This can be a good time to get away from it all. You may want to get on with some private activities out of everyone's way. Or you can find this a good time for a retreat for spiritual or other reasons. Various spiritual disciplines such as yoga and meditation are likely to help you feel more calm and centered. Family matters will be more peaceful than usual.

Weekly Summary

A little bout of traveling can come up for many of you this week. You may find that a partner can do with a change. Or you yourself may be in need of a break from business and household activities. Those of you who are keen on sports will find it worth a long trip to see a favorite team. Leo students may have to meet a teacher. This can be most helpful in getting your interest in your studies back again.

Work schedules will be quite exacting for you just now. But you will be able to deal with a variety of problems involving people and situations. You can find that dealing with the public is no cup of tea. People seem to be ready to complain and be stubborn at the drop of a hat. You will need to keep your tolerance and sense of humor going so that you can ride above it all. This will be a good time for making money from artistic professional activities.

Be prepared to meet some odd people after the weekend at a social function. You can be dealing with groups of foreigners in various ways. You will have a lot going for you socially. Old friends may turn up from your past and surprise you. You can be calm and steady despite all the turmoil around you.

26th Week/June 25–July 1

Thursday the 25th. You can feel the need for some space physically and mentally. A lot of good and intuitive ideas can keep coming up. A charity event will do well with fund-raising. Spiritual groups you attend can help you and a partner to heal a rift. You may feel very anxious about a work matter, but a lot of it can be in your imagination rather than in reality.

Friday the 26th. You tend to be full of reforming zeal. This is fine if you are working on self-transformation, but it will not be so funny if you try to change others as well. You can exude a lot of charisma and attraction for others. A partner or lover can get a bit possessive about all this. Power struggles can occur between you and a friend.

Saturday the 27th. A cheerful and energetic attitude will get you a long way this weekend. You can enjoy a great many lively social cvents and activities. Working out in a gym can do you a lot of good. You are likely to be in the mood for some physical action. This can be a good day for making a very personal decision. A warmhearted friend can do you a lot of good.

Sunday the 28th. Pleasures and entertainment can become a trifle costly at times. You can enjoy a very expensive meal out tonight but may have to foot the bill. The day will be good for any kind of private work. You may be able to recoup your losses by doing some extra work early or working through your breaks. You may hear of a new job through the grapevine.

Monday the 29th. Some taxes might have to be paid now. You can find that a child needs outfitting in a major way. There can be a few emotional scenes with a lover when out together. Jealousy seems to be the cause of your problems. You may need to get a secret deal organized for your business or firm. Things may still have to be hush-hush, especially if you are dealing with foreign enterprises.

Tuesday the 30th. A spendthrift streak in you now can make you careless with money. You tend to be impulsive at times. A friend may get quite angry with something you say early in the day. You may need to apologize and be a bit more sensitive about certain issues. In many ways, this can turn out to be a lucky time. But you will need to follow your intuition to get things right.

Wednesday July 1st. This is likely to be a very favorable day for dealings with others. You can enjoy a dinner party with your local friends. Above all, you can get involved in some interesting and informative conversation. There may be a problem with a brother or sister. Relatives generally appear to be in need of some sympathy and compassion.

Weekly Summary

You will find that dealing with powerful people brings out the best in you. This can be a good week for sorting out your own personal needs and interests. You will have lots of energy and feel better prepared to assert yourself in a positive way. You may discover a lot about yourself through hobbies and other creative activities you are engaged in. Just now, you are in the mood for physical activities and interests; these may include some sort of team sports.

You will have to keep a careful eye on your generous nature this week. Financial interests can vary a good deal. You may find that an impulsive action costs you dear. However, there will be a lot of luck in the air as well. So keep your eyes open and awake to whatever is going on. Take care not to overexpand a business or to be too trusting of a friend's promises. Some issue can get blown out of all proportion.

This is likely to be a good time for meetings with neighbors or other local friends. You can enjoy a party or other entertainment together. A local charity will be more than glad of your help or simply some new ideas for summer activities and fund-raising.

27th Week/July 2–8

Thursday the 2nd. This may turn out to be one of those frustrating and irritating days. Too many responsibilities at work will make you feel strained and tired. Be careful not to overexert yourself physically. You can misjudge your strength. A group meeting tonight can get a bit upsetting at times. Your patience with a friend may be used up fast.

Friday the 3rd. It will be advisable to be as open as you can with someone at work. You can find that family members are in need of some practical help. You may need to comfort them if they are in trouble. Elderly parents or relatives may get in touch. Try not to feel too burdened with all these problems. It will be wise to ask other family members to help out as well.

Saturday the 4th. This Independence Day can be a good time to visit someone in a hospital or home. You need to be very much aware of a partner's feelings in a difficult situation. Some of you may be considering retirement soon. You can find a family powwow very helpful when making a far-reaching decision. A dinner date tonight will prove to be very romantic and exciting for new lovers.

Sunday the 5th. This will be a much happier morning for family matters. You can feel very fortunate and glad to be surrounded by all your loved ones. Property issues may need to be discussed with care. Some of you may be considering a move some way off or even overseas. A house or garden will need some work on it. Putting up an extension can give you all a lot more freedom and space.

Monday the 6th. A determination to get a creative project finished can keep you at it now. You can enjoy any form of self-expression. Theater and writing are usually favorites of you Leo people. You and a loved one can enjoy a trip away. You are sure to find that a child is really changing your life. A baby may produce its first word or start walking.

Tuesday the 7th. Be wary of others trying to take you for a ride. You can be gullible over money matters at times. This is not a good time to go in for risky speculative ventures or gambles. You can have a lot of fun. You may, in fact, get a little bit wild at times. However, it can do you good to let your hair down now and then. A lover can be a bit smothering or overbearing.

Wednesday the 8th. Everyday activities will need some careful attention right now. You are ready to buckle down and be disciplined about things. Take time to relax though, for you can drive yourself too hard. You tend to be erratic in your energies. Workmates may be unhelpful. A lot of unexpected events can really throw out your planned schedule for the day.

Weekly Summary

You may find that family situations are rather confusing this week. It will be a good idea to keep out of things as much as you can until you can see just what is going on. If you are considering a move, wait a little while before making any positive decisions. You can find that a sympathetic attitude toward relatives isn't always the best move. They may take advantage of your kindness.

The weekend will turn out to be more fun than expected. You can be in top form and ready for some stimulating and interesting get-togethers with loved ones. Teaching children can bring out all your latent talents. You are likely to find that new ideas and interests get you going on some new creative projects. In fact, this will be likely to be a quite inspired time. You will need to watch a tendency to have too many irons in the fire.

Dealing with your usual day-to-day activities can keep you pretty busy after the weekend. You seem to have a lot of things to do at work. It may feel at times as if you are soldiering on alone. Co-workers just seem to be wasting time or may be away on sick leave.

28th Week/July 9–15

Thursday the 9th. You may have some problems with a sick child. However, you can be a model of patience at times. Your own health will tend to worry you. It may be a good idea to consult a doctor or other specialist and set your mind at rest. Perhaps you will need to have some work done on your teeth. A boss may seem to be acting behind your back.

Friday the 10th. Things will be a lot easier to deal with this morning. Get all your usual daily activities done early; get them all finished and out of the way. You may be getting a bit more cooperation from fellow workers. In fact you can feel quite expansive and jolly with everyone. The afternoon can be tiring, but there should be a sense of satisfaction about it.

Saturday the 11th. A partner's odd reaction to a proposal can tend to throw you a bit. You may really have felt you put things over with tact and charm, only to be rebuffed. This can be a good time for such social events as parties and dinner dates. You will enjoy dancing with a loved one. Dealing with youngsters may be tough at times.

Sunday the 12th. This can be a good day for helping with some charitable matter. You seem prepared to work away from the limelight for a minimal fee. You may have to clarify some tax matter on a creative project that has been selling well. This will be a good day for making important decisions on a public situation. You may need to deal with some important officials.

Monday the 13th. You can spend this day quietly, particularly if you are in the retail business. There may be a lull in the usual rush of people. This can leave you some time to get on with taking stock, sorting out accounts, and other joint financial matters. Those in therapy may have little to say. You will feel a little anxious about something for no apparent reason.

Tuesday the 14th. You will really be in luck financially now. But don't go out and splurge just like that. It's true, you will feel generous toward loved ones and want them to have a good time. For instance, you may want to show your gratitude to friends by asking them out to a meal. Parties can be great fun and may have their romantic moments. A journey to some exotic place may start late tonight.

Wednesday the 15th. A lively day can be spent traveling around. A sudden impulse can take you visiting your in-laws. A partner may be a bit eccentric at times. However, you will feel warm and friendly together. All the same, the day will not be without its arguments over various points of view. Meeting unusual people will make travel exciting. Students can do very well.

Weekly Summary

You will try hard to catch up with your everyday needs and activities. However, you may be called away from these to deal with sick relatives, pets, or children. Or you may find that you are not really functioning at your best yourself. However, if you slow your pace and keep your patience, you can achieve a lot more than you hoped. Friday can be a good day for dealing with all you have planned both at home and at work. It does help when staff and co-workers are ready to pull their weight.

A partner is sure to be in a friendly and relaxed mood over the weekend. You may be trying to explain something that is important to you to others, but at times it can be hard to get your message across. You need to persevere. Don't let work get in the way of having a good time with loved ones. People are always more important than things.

This can be a good time for getting to grips with various corporate money matters. This will be necessary if the time has come to sort out various tax or insurance concerns. You may have a little lull on Monday. This will give you time to see what is happening and make any necessary adjustments.

29th Week/July16–22

Thursday the 16th. You may get a bit carried away by a guru figure. Be as detached and down to earth as you can. Don't believe all you hear. A boss may ask you to make a special trip on his behalf early in the day. While this can be very enjoyable, it can set you back with your own work. You will feel vague and dreamy in the afternoon.

Friday the 17th. You can now get on well with professional matters. You may find that a partner wants to make a few radical changes. You can act the hypocrite with a friend or at a function you attend. However, this may be a wise move if you have certain things to hide. A lawyer or counselor may have unorthodox ways of dealing with your problems.

Saturday the 18th. If you have a lot to say at work, get it off your chest. You can tend to be very chatty with a special client. The day will be good for doing business with a foreigner, especially in property or shares. You can be very lucky with a little private deal you are making. A partner may have a really inspired idea for an evening out.

Sunday the 19th. If you try to be too domineering with a child, you can arouse a lot of resentment. Try to be more friendly and detached about a certain issue. A counselor can help you get to the bottom of some childhood problem. You may find that a friend or lover is acting in a jealous and possessive manner. Do not retaliate; keep yourself calm.

Monday the 20th. You can really enjoy yourself with some friends. This can be a time when certain influential individuals will cooperate with you well. You should be able to come up with a few really good ideas at a business meeting. However, it may be important to think through the details before they can be made viable. You will feel confident and cheerful.

Tuesday the 21st. You can enjoy the morning with a loved one. A meeting will go well, especially if you are planning fund-raising activities. You can get down to some work by yourself later in the day. You seem to be well organized, and you intend to get a good deal done at home or through overtime. Your enthusiasm will be strong about a professional matter but tempered by caution.

Wednesday the 22nd. It isn't always easy to relax. However, you now can be calm and quite laid-back. You may enjoy meeting a friend or an old flame from the past. Dealing with a pension issue can occupy your day. You might have to meet with certain officials. They can be very helpful and polite. This will be a good day for those who have a lot of shopping to do.

Weekly Summary

Your career can be very busy and exhausting at present. There seem to be a lot of demands on your time and energy. Important decisions may have to be made behind closed doors as far as a particular partnership is concerned. It seems one of you may want out, or at least may want some radical changes made. Make sure that you discuss all the angles together before coming to any conclusions. You should be enjoying your professional life. It certainly appears to be remunerative at present.

Be sure to give yourself some space when a friend or a group starts to put the pressure on you. These people may want to make use of your creative talents in some way. While this is all very nice and ego-boosting, you need to be sure you get a fair deal. A lover seems to be acting in an emotional fashion. Don't let it get to you. Just keep detached and friendly.

You can end this week taking some time off for a private enterprise or venture. You may simply be in need of some time off alone to work on a few new schemes and ideas. It can also be a good time for a retreat or a short vacation with a loved one. There are times we all need to be left in peace for a bit.

30th Week/July 23–29

Thursday the 23rd. As far as your own personal needs and interests are concerned, this can be a day to make a fresh start. You can feel a little disillusioned by a mate or spouse. Be wary when dealing with a lawyer or business partner, who does not appear to be acting in a straightforward manner. You can feel very over-burdened with professional problems at times.

Friday the 24th. Now will be time to take stock of your own needs and desires. You can enjoy having a day all to yourself to do your own thing. Have a massage, a workout in the gym, or some beauty treatment. Pamper yourself with luxury for a day. You are sure to feel better for it. Others will be ready to leave you in peace and make no demands. Make the most of it.

Saturday the 25th. The morning can be a good time for giving a talk or taking over a meeting. You will be in fine form and ready to convince all of your particular ideas. Later in the day, you may need to sort out some financial matter. Your own earnings will be steady and regular now. You can be very well organized when out shopping.

Sunday the 26th. This can be a very good day for earning ready money. You may be involved in raising funds through various sponsored activities or other charitable ventures. Although you may want to do a good deal, you will not feel physically up to a lot. You can feel a little low at times, maybe even with a sense of having failed at something. Don't let a superior put you down.

Monday the 27th. You may be inclined to spend too much. Buying large, maybe luxurious, items may have to be curbed. You can be reckless on a speculative matter. This is not a good time for expanding a business. Try not to be so rash and overconfident. Check out all the details first. You may feel a letdown about a contract.

Tuesday the 28th. This will be a very favorable time for educational matters. Winding up a course can give you a real sense of satisfaction, whether you are a teacher or a student. A special neighbor can change your life in some way. You may feel that a good long talk with a mate or a lover can sort out some of your hidden emotional issues.

Wednesday the 29th. Be a little less impulsive; try not to rush about too much. You may be heading for a car accident if you do. You may be obliged to go to see a neighbor or relative in the hospital. Something or someone can make you hopping mad. However, it will be wise to be tactful and make a few compromises and just fume secretly.

Weekly Summary

This can be your week if you want to make something of it. There can be some good opportunities to put your personal plans and ideas into action, especially on Thursday. In fact, you may be inclined to make a whole new start. This can mean a divorce or breakup for some of you Leo people. You seem a little unsure about a partnership matter. In fact, you may feel sad and disillusioned at times.

A lot of active effort will be put into fund-raising this weekend. You will be in a generous and even a reckless mood with your money just now. Don't be carried away by optimism or false credibility. Someone you have trusted can let you down severely. You may have a real spending spree on Monday. Be sure you don't buy things you will later regret, as your taste tends toward the gaudy just now.

Neighbors will tend to be a mixed blessing this week. You can find a special relationship developing with someone in your local area. But you may be inclined to go full steam ahead without thinking things through with care. Beware of speaking out of turn and landing yourself in hot water on Wednesday.

31st Week/July 30–August 5

Thursday the 30th. If you chair a meeting this morning, you will make sure that your own viewpoint is represented. This can be a good time to put forward several personal plans and schemes. Local matters and educational issues will be of importance. You will need to watch that a partner's anxiety isn't getting through to you. A lot may just be imaginary.

Friday the 31st. You can be at odds with a parent or an elder child. Be as detached as you can when someone is behaving in a very contradictory manner. You can enjoy some peace and quiet in your own den or study later in the day. Listening to music, looking at beautiful pictures, or visiting a museum can all be soothing to your soul. You can feel a real need to be at home.

Saturday August 1st. This is likely to be a happy and successful day for family matters. You may not feel much in the mood for conversation. Being with the family, puttering about the house or in the garden will be relaxing and make you feel good. You can find that a recent extension to the home gives you all a lot of space. You may have lots of ideas for future improvements to be made.

Sunday the 2nd. You and a mate seem determined to enjoy yourselves. You may feel like going to see a mystery play or a thriller at the movies. You are not likely to be in the mood for light drama. An unusual experience with a lover can be very exciting. You seem to be very confident in your powers of attraction just now. A child can give you a lot of pleasure and entertaining antics.

Monday the 3rd. Unusual activities can keep you and a partner busy. You may not be able to agree on a lot of things. Your need to be creative can follow some different paths. The advice of a lover can give you some fresh ideas for a hobby or other interest. Children may be acting in a very awkward and clumsy fashion. You will need a lot of patience to deal with them.

Tuesday the 4th. Those of you who are involved in writing and publishing work will find things going well in this field. However, you may have more of a financial outlay than expected. The morning can be a very good time for creative matters. A lot of your grander ideas may seem ready to be fulfilled. Keep a sense of proportion all the same. You should get a good deal organized at work later.

Wednesday the 5th. If you keep a low profile, you can get through a lot of your routine work. Any backlog can then be sorted out, making you feel well organized and efficient. Health matters may need to be dealt with on your own behalf or that of others. Basically this can be a quiet and ordinary day. You will feel bored at times, but you will plod on.

Weekly Summary

Home matters can be very delightful at times this week. If you have been redecorating, building extensions, or otherwise improving things, you will feel well satisfied. You may feel like making home your retreat at times. Family members seem to be on good terms now. But you can still have the odd dustup with a parental figure. You may find that an older child is spreading wings and ready to leave the nest.

The weekend ought to be a very enjoyable time for you. You will be in the mood to get out and about and have some fun in your own inimitable way. A partner's opinions don't seem to count that much. The day will be good for dealing with creative matters. You can enjoy getting on with hobbies and other interests. In fact, a wide variety of activity is what you mostly seem to need just now. All the same, try not to make too many plans that cannot be fulfilled.

After your various weekend entertainment and enjoyments, it can be time to get down to the nitty-gritty of routine work and tasks about the home. You are sure to be well organized and can soon catch up on any backlog. Your health will be stable, but try not to eat spicy foods that upset your stomach.

32nd Week/August 6–12

Thursday the 6th. You should have a good morning for getting on with your workaday activities. It will feel as if things are rolling along quite effortlessly by themselves. You will be in good health and pleased with the outcome of a work matter. Later in the day, you may have some trouble sorting out a partner's problems. The person can be anxious and a bit sorry for himself or herself.

Friday the 7th. If you can find a new approach to a legal matter, you will be wise to pursue it. This is not an easy time for relationships. It can be the end of the road for some of you Leo people. However, others may find new ways of approaching old problems. Try to be detached. Don't assume you are always in the right. You may feel very restless at times.

Saturday the 8th. If you have some problems to discuss with a partner, take the time to get it all off your chest. You can be very argumentative and keep on taking the opposite view. Admit that some of your ideas are a bit farfetched or eccentric. You may have to deal with some difficult or rebellious youngsters. You can be tense and irritable at times.

Sunday the 9th. This will not be an easy day for sorting out family financial matters. If people are trying to have a struggle of wills, you may just decide to call their bluff. And there's no prize for guessing who wins. You are not in a mood for compromise at all. An inheritance can cause some emotional problems. A lover's possessive attitude may make you feel threatened and trapped.

Monday the 10th. This ought to be a very fortunate time for you Leo people. You may be enjoying a secret romance. You tend to be very altruistic where money is concerned. It can be a day for spending lavishly on loved ones. You may have a quiet and private dinner with a loved one, and this will make you feel very happy. It will be a good day for spiritual activities, although you may not want to talk about these with just anyone.

Tuesday the 11th. You and a lover can have a really cheerful day together. Intense encounters with a partner can bring a lot of feelings to the surface. Children may need to be kept under control. The best way is to keep them amused and on the go. A trip to somewhere quite different can be very exciting and stimulating. You may find that your life is changed for the better in many ways.

Wednesday the 12th. In some respects this can be a rather stressful day. You will tend to try to pack in a lot of activity. Water sports may figure high on your list if you are on vacation. You will enjoy a journey very much. You may have to be in charge of a group of young people, but you seem to know just how to deal with them successfully. A special individual can teach you a good deal spiritually.

Weekly Summary

It can be tough getting others to see things your way this week. In fact, for some of you, it will appear that differences of opinion with a partner are too wide a gulf to breach. Take a hard look at what is going on. Maybe you are being too dogmatic or self-righteous at times. You certainly are very powerful at the moment and not likely to let anyone stand in your way. Naturally this can provoke some real ego clashes.

You may have to look at a corporate or family financial situation this weekend. Not everything may be going according to plan. You may be trying to get some expensive hobby off the ground. Or a creative venture can need some financial backing that is not forthcoming. It will be worth persevering and pushing to get things going. Things can change quite rapidly by Monday. In fact, you can find Fortune smiling on you very nicely.

A short trip or journey you make from Tuesday on can turn out to be very successful. Those of you on vacation will now get a chance to participate in all those water sports you have been dreaming about. Others of you may just want to enjoy yourselves in your own special and private way.

33rd Week/August 13–19

Thursday the 13th. You can have some problems when a partner refuses to support a professional move. You may be trying to break free from a certain relationship. However, a mate or spouse may not be willing to let go. This can be a day for disillusionment. You may have idealized someone too much. Now you may come face-to-face with reality.

Friday the 14th. A meeting at work can put you in a very optimistic frame of mind. If you are in charge of others, be sure to let them have their say about a project. A superior may have a useful tip for a financial deal. You will be very eager and enthusiastic about a private enterprise. It may be time to expand a business and put your assets to good use.

Saturday the 15th. You can have a pleasant evening out. A lover will be very intense and very passionate. Romantic prospects can be very exciting now. You will be full of energy and very cheerful. Your charm and wit will really bowl a partner over. A major professional decision can mean a lot to you careerwise. Luck will be on your side, but take time and don't rush.

Sunday the 16th. You can use your charm to control someone or a situation. A public appearance may not come off as well as you were hoping. You may feel like keeping yourself to yourself. However, you will have certain duties to perform that mean getting on with it. You can give a very interesting talk or speech to a group of people with whom you are involved.

Monday the 17th. There can be a few tasks to catch up on that may mean staying at home. If an elderly person is ill, you may have to take that person to the hospital or go visit him or her in a home. An official can help you out behind the scenes. You may find that a lover is really charmed by your style. You will have a powerful effect on others and will mean to use it.

Tuesday the 18th. This can turn out to be a very quiet day indeed. You may decide to go on a retreat for a day or two. Or you may simply need to withdraw from life's hustle and bustle. It will be a good time for spiritual reading, yoga, and meditation. Those of you who are retired may feel a bit bored with it all. Others are likely to be glad of a break.

Wednesday the 19th. You will feel very free and open with others. It can be a good time just to do things your own way and by yourself. You can really feel the need for some space. However, by the afternoon your need for others may reassert itself. Then you may start complaining that no one is calling you up. A work matter can be demanding. You may feel anxious about the outcome.

Weekly Summary

A professional situation may come under review this week. You will be doing very well these days and should be feeling secure and stable on the whole. However, this can be a time when things can begin to get in a bit of a rut. So check with a partner or work colleague. You can find ways of making improvements and adding some interest and incentive to the work. A public meeting will only enhance people's appreciation of your talents.

Enjoy a varied social round at the weekend. You seem to have some different places to go to and unusual people to meet. In fact, for some of you, an exciting little flirtation can add some romantic spice to your fare. You will be in a mood to please and be pleased, to charm and be charmed. Generally your spirits will be high; you can meet with equally lively friends. Between you, you can paint the town red.

After all the excitement of your weekend and social happenings, you may withdraw to some extent from the public gaze. You may be obliged to visit someone unwell or in an institution. You will be quite ready to do your duty and take it as it comes. Any spiritual work or disciplines will be favored.

34th Week/August 20–26

Thursday the 20th. No one can gainsay a Leo when in a sweet and charming mood, and there is no doubt that you can be very lovable these days. However, a partner still may refuse to cooperate, but you can be ready to forgive. You may need to watch your health. A headache or backache can seem to come from nowhere. Be sure you aren't just holding in a lot of tension.

Friday the 21st. Now can be a time to make a fresh start with a very personal situation. You can decide that enough is enough and make a break from someone very trying. You will enjoy wearing unusual clothes. Maybe you are determined to make a statement about yourself, but be sure that it isn't too outrageous. A rebellious streak in you can lead you to challenge a superior.

Saturday the 22nd. If you are careful with an inheritance or tax refund, you can put some aside for a rainy day. However, you may find that some of your assets have to be plowed back for your professional needs. A lover may try to be too controlling. You will have to be more stern with a child who is rude or unpleasant.

Sunday the 23rd. Be ready to take off financially. You are really comfortably off just now. This can be a good time to go on a shopping spree and buy some large items you have longed for. Your values are sure to be important to you. You can be very optimistic about the future. Buying a larger property will look like a good idea after all.

Monday the 24th. Your compassion and sympathy can be aroused this morning. You may want to take care of someone who is ill. A pet can bring out the best in you. You may find that a co-worker is very kind when you are in need. Later in the day, you may have an energetic or heated discussion with a neighbor. You will really have to stand your ground.

Tuesday the 25th. You are likely to be in a relaxed and happy frame of mind. A gossip with a neighbor can be fun. A love letter or romantic phone call can make you feel really loved and wanted. It will be a very favorable day for traveling around the local area. You may find some real beauty spots to visit. A good book can capture your attention.

Wednesday the 26th. Although this can be a quiet day in many ways, you may feel a bit discontented. You seem to be a bit low in energy right now, even listless. Maybe you are bored with your work and the sameness of it all. However, you can pick up the phone and exchange sweet nothings with a loved one. Take care not to overdo any physical activity.

Weekly Summary

This should be a promising week for any personal ventures and interests. You will also find that relationship issues are vastly improved. Much of this may be due to the fact that you are in top form and especially charming and attractive. You can make a completely new start now on a highly personal issue. This will definitely be the time for turning over a new leaf. You may even want to dress differently and create a whole new image.

You may have a few hassles with a financial matter. Those of you who are self-employed should set some cash aside for tax purposes. Maybe this is the time to consider an insurance policy or make a will. You still may be quite gullible about certain corporate deals. Or maybe you simply are being careless and trusting too much to your good luck.

You can have some interesting talks with a loved one. You will be inclined toward reading and thinking of beautiful and peaceful things. You really will not be in the mood to get all wound up over anything. Local matters will proceed smoothly. Journeys to local places of beauty and interest can be very pleasant.

35th Week/August 27–September 2

Thursday the 27th. This can be a tense and tiring day. You can waste a lot of energy battling over something with a mate. Sudden disruptive events in the family are likely to be upsetting. You may feel very angry when a partner makes changes behind your back. Take care when working in the house or yard, as you are likely to be prone to accidents.

Friday the 28th. You may feel really fed up about some recent family news. It may be hard to be pleasant to an erring relative. You can be having some conflict of opinion over an inheritance matter. A lover will try hard to cheer you up. You will have an enjoyable time with a child. In fact, this can transform your day and help you to regain your good spirits.

Saturday the 29th. Taking a more compassionate and sympathetic attitude toward a family member can help to change the situation. You can be a lot more forgiving. The afternoon can be happily spent with a lover. You will enjoy being active together. Children will tend to be noisy and full of high spirits. You may be a bit domineering at times. Try not to push your own needs first.

Sunday the 30th. Things will really change for the better. This can turn out to be a day for doing some exciting and quite different things. A partner will have a few innovative ideas up his or her sleeve. You will enjoy going to the theater. Creative interests or hobbies can be far better if shared with a loved one. You may be seized with sudden inspiration creatively.

Monday the 31st. Turning your ideas of beauty into creative interests can produce some fine results. You may attempt to do too much. Or you can find that entertaining a lot of children is a costly affair. This can, however, be a good day for a kiddies' birthday party or other fun thing. You will feel very happy with a loved one. You may spend a lot on some special clothes.

Tuesday September 1st. A boss will be a good deal more helpful than usual. You will be very well organized at work. If you have to take charge of others, everything will go smoothly and well. You are likely to be in good health right now. You may be taking more interest than usual in medical and health matters, which may lead you to spend a lot of money on vitamins and other diet supplements.

Wednesday the 2nd. This can be a very happy and cheerful day. You are likely to be absorbed in various routine jobs at home or at work. But you will be very contented with what you are doing. Things should flow well and with ease. Co-workers and staff will be good-humored and ready to pull their weight. You can enjoy being with pets, especially dogs and horses.

Weekly Summary

Although family matters can leave a lot to be desired this week, you will end up feeling a little more at ease and contented with things by Friday morning. A relative, especially a brother or sister, may be quite demanding or difficult at times. You may be very eager to persuade a partner to make a few changes in the home or garden. But this can be where you come up against a spot of real opposition.

This can be the time to get out of the house and away from the family hurly-burly. Use the weekend to get out and about on the town. Maybe a real change of activity and some fun can act like a tonic to edgy nerves. Going to the theater generally appeals to you Leo people. So try something musical or attractive that can take you out of the humdrum. You will also be in a very inspired and creative mood this weekend, which will favor those interested in arts or music.

Your daily routine will be moving along very smoothly and beautifully this week. You can enjoy being in charge of things at work. In fact, this usually brings out the best in you. Co-workers will seem to be in a very good humor and cooperative too. Your health should be particularly good right now.

36th Week/September 3–9

Thursday the 3rd. You may be a little annoyed about a situation at work. Things can be constantly changing and messing up your well-planned routines. You will need to keep your wits about you, as well as a sense of humor. The day will be good for dealing with children or with creative matters. You will need to keep your spirit of rebellion in check when dealing with an official.

Friday the 4th. It isn't easy to talk things over when a mate or spouse refuses to listen. You may feel as if you are banging your head against a brick wall. You may be explosive and bad-tempered, but this is because you are under some sort of strain. A counselor or legal adviser may have some bad news that affects you or your children.

Saturday the 5th. You need to sort out your assets and see what can be salvaged from a deal that misfired. You need to take care not to gamble with other people's money. This will not be an easy time for dealing with a child's emotional problems. You may well feel you have troubles enough of your own. A tax official or the police may need to see you about some matter.

Sunday the 6th. It may feel as if Fortune has stopped smiling on you of late. This is likely to turn out to be a day for various confrontations with a member of the opposite sex. You may be quarreling over money matters. However, as you haven't entirely lost your sense of humor or proportion, you should be able to come to some agreement, or at least a cease-fire.

Monday the 7th. You may feel quite spaced-out this Labor Day, but this will not prevent you doing some good work. You can enjoy photography or filming if this is part of your daily activity. Going to someone for healing or therapy may work well but can seem a bit pricey. A partner may have a change of mind over a journey you meant to take.

Tuesday the 8th. If you have to go traveling, things will be quiet and uneventful. You may, of course, be very glad of this. An in-law is likely to be in touch and can be warm and cheerful. You can relax when on vacation, as there will be little to do. This can be a good time to consider your plans for future studies and courses.

Wednesday the 9th. Professional interests can revolve around various money issues. If you are dealing with property, this can be a very good day for you. There may be contracts to sign. But be careful to read all the fine print. You may be anxious about the outcome of an official inquiry. Shopping, especially if you are interested in cars, computers, or telephone equipment, will be rewarding.

Weekly Summary

These days, you seem to have problems making a partner understand just how you feel. However, blowing your top will not really help to get your point across either. You may find that subtle persuasion can do a lot more. Problems concerning children and their custody can feature in divorce cases. You may find that a lawyer or counselor has some very different ways of dealing with things. You are likely to feel quite tense this week.

It may be a good idea to have all the documents ready for an official inquiry. Then you need not be caught napping at the last minute. Although this will be a strained and tense week in many areas, you can still keep a grip on it all. The weekend can be devoted to sorting out corporate or family money matters. You may have to work on a property issue as well. Children will also need to be prepared with all their supplies for school, which can be a financial worry too.

You may have to sort out some of your own needs if you are soon to start a new course of study somewhere. There can be a lot to consider and discuss. You may have to see an official about a passport or visa matter before going away.

37th Week/September 10–16

Thursday the 10th. You may get into a bit of a panic at work. There really will seem to be a lot to get through. However, luck will be on your side. Things can get a bit manic at times when dealing with the public. Your sense of humor and cheerful attitude will help to keep everyone laughing. A loved one may phone you and cheer you up. This can be a good time to buy a car.

Friday the 11th. Take things slowly and carefully this morning. You can meet up with someone glamorous. The day will be good for those involved in healing or spiritual work. The afternoon may see you having some problems with a youngster. You may find that a lover is being very demanding and jealous when you go out together. You will find this behavior most upsetting.

Saturday the 12th. A good time can be had by all tonight. This will be a good day for social events and activities. You will feel very energetic and lively. An influential person may prove to be a real bore, with very materialistic values. If a boss is acting in a critical and dismissive manner, you can laugh it off rather than get mad.

Sunday the 13th. This can be a steady and quiet day for you. You may enjoy more earnest and philosophical activities than usual. Some of you will find a retreat or spiritual weekend very calming and good for you. Those involved in yoga and meditation will be more disciplined and eager to get on with it. The day will be good for any public matter; you will take your duties responsibly and seriously.

Monday the 14th. You will be very relaxed and at peace. A brother or sister can be very good company and have some good news. You can enjoy just being alone with your thoughts. Some of you may be dreaming up ways of making a little private cash on the side. Go to see people in the hospital. You can have a very soothing effect on others.

Tuesday the 15th. This morning is likely to be a lucky and a cheerful time. You can find that a bank officer or other financial adviser is ready to make allowances and help you out. A private property deal should work out in your favor. You will be in a sympathetic mood toward those who are not well. Someone in a home will be delighted to have a visit from you.

Wednesday the 16th. You can feel quite changed toward someone. You may feel you have only just begun to know the person. A partner can have some very good ideas for a joint creative venture. You may have to give it all some careful thought. You will tend to be erratic in your attitudes toward a child. But then you seem to be getting a lot of flak and rebelliousness from them just now.

Weekly Summary

You may find that a professional matter needs some discussing, especially if you need extra help with it financially. You seem to be very energetic and eager to get something off the ground. Try not to be too impulsive or rush into something. It will be wise to consult an expert or specialist. You may have all sorts of brain-waves up your sleeve, too many sometimes.

You appear to be having some problems keeping a child or lover from showing you up socially. This will really make you furious on Friday. You can take a lot of flak, but bad behavior is intolerable. This can be a rather stressful time if you are involved with some political group. You can feel as if you are being pressured into things you really don't want to do. Stand your ground. A friendship can get a bit rocky over the weekend.

Take a little time off from the mainstream of life to consider what your next move should be. You may need to give thought to career and financial matters above all. This can also be the sort of time when you feel more interest in spiritual matters. You can be bountiful and jolly toward someone who is ill and may be in the hospital.

38th Week/September 17–23

Thursday the 17th. It may be a good idea to use a fairly quiet day like this to work out any personal plans you have. These can be mainly creative ones, or you may want to think up ways of getting yourself noticed by others. You can reappraise your whole image. Is it the real you? Take time off for a beauty treatment or a hair styling that brings out the best in you.

Friday the 18th. If you are finding it hard work dealing with accounts and taxes and other money matters, see an expert and ask for help. You seem to have shouldered a lot of responsibilities of late. You should find that regular earnings are helping you to pay off a few old debts. You can get a lot organized and dealt with, but you don't really seem to be enjoying yourself.

Saturday the 19th. This can be a good day for those who deal in bulk. You should be able to get your hands on all the right commodities. If you are interested in cars, computers, and so on, you may find some real bargains. Keep an eye on the details of any contract you are asked to sign. A business meeting can see the satisfactory conclusion of a deal.

Sunday the 20th. If you attend a spiritual meeting, you may feel you have acquired some new way of looking at life. Perhaps your values seem to be too material or unrealistic. You can have a lot of ideas buzzing about in your head. Using your money toward more philanthropic ends may be one. You can enjoy driving a new car and really showing off in it.

Monday the 21st. This will be quite an exciting day for you and a partner. You can enjoy various little shopping trips and other amusements in your local area. A surprise invitation from a neighbor can be a change from your usual routine. Students may enjoy meeting unusual people or studying subjects that are quite different. Observance of Rosh Hashanah may be the highlight of the day.

Tuesday the 22nd. You will be bouncing with energy. Physical activities can be fun and do you good. You can enjoy taking part in local team sports. Although there will be a lot of work to get through, you can keep going in a methodical and careful fashion. This will be particularly helpful to those of you who are writers or teachers. You are likely to be more sensitive to detail than usual.

Wednesday the 23rd. If you are too scattered in your thinking, you can undo all the good you have done previously. Work this morning can be confused and chaotic at times. Later on, you may try to get things in order. However, a family matter may have to be dealt with first. You can take a course in healing or photography. This may help you with your work eventually.

Weekly Summary

Take care when dealing with your personal finances this week. You can do very well as long as you keep to necessities and avoid luxuries for the present. This can be a time when paying off accumulated debts can lead to a release and freedom from past problems. This will be a good week for buying, either for a business or for personal reasons. You may have various schemes and dreams for using cash you have put aside.

You will find that neighbors are ready to be quite friendly and forthcoming. This can help you to take more interest in local matters and activities. You may be involved in some sort of fund-raising for a local project or charity. This can mean that you are prepared to help out with time and money if necessary. However, there may not be that much of either available just now. You may want to go out on a few local trips for shopping purposes.

Don't take on all the family burdens. Dealing with an older person may need the help of a brother or sister. You will tend to work hard in order to help keep up a standard of living. An air of sacrifice is fine, but it may make others feel guilty. Maybe you should rebel a little and ask a partner to pull his or her weight.

39th Week/September 24–30

Thursday the 24th. Although a property matter can be going ahead, it may be costing you a lot more than you expected in legal fees and so on. You may feel like decorating a home or adding an extension to it. Be sure to get several estimates first. You may find that someone in the family has grossly exaggerated certain problems. A loved one may shower you with gifts.

Friday the 25th. Be considerate of a family member. You will find that a more sensitive approach is the best this morning. A home by the sea may fulfill a dream for you. You can enjoy some peace and quiet in your home or puttering in the garden. The afternoon may be spent with a neighbor. You can meet an influential person in your local area.

Saturday the 26th. This will be a good day to spend with a mate or spouse. You can be ready to do some enjoyable things and let up on all the work you have been doing. You may have a sudden creative binge. You can feel all sorts of good ideas bubbling up inside you now. Children may do some strange things, but they will be lively and active and full of fun. Why not join them?

Sunday the 27th. You may get a bit carried away at times with a theatrical production. You may be involved in some musical or artistic venture. It will be a good day for psychology studies. You may become very absorbed in reading crime fiction or watching a thriller on TV. Generally it will be a good day for just enjoying yourself. You can feel in an impulsive mood at times.

Monday the 28th. Daily tasks and interests can be boring but necessary. With a little organization and discipline, you can get through things quite quickly. This can leave you with some time free for your own interests and plans. A neighbor may have some good ideas for getting out with the kids and enjoying yourselves. You will be in a chatty and cheerful frame of mind.

Tuesday the 29th. This is likely to be a very good day for getting on with practical everyday things. You will enjoy the company of co-workers. Jokes and good humor can make time pass more pleasantly. A surprise invitation from a neighborhood friend may be forthcoming. You may receive a message from a legal adviser that can change a situation completely.

Wednesday the 30th. You will need to be aware of subtle influences at work. Someone may need sympathy. You will be in an idealistic mood and can feel attracted to somebody new. However, a sense of duty to a partner will make you behave yourself. Those of you involved in healing will be able to help a lot of sick people. The religious holiday will put some Leos in a solemn mood.

Weekly Summary

You will feel lazy about the house and garden this week. Getting down to some of the little details may be all you feel like doing. You may be considering how to improve the property. Maybe an extension or a re-decorating plan is in mind, but it can still be at the dreaming and planning stage. You are likely to be very sympathetic toward family members. In fact, you may even have to take care of someone just now.

This can be a good weekend for creative interests and various hobbies. You seem to have a lot of plans and ideas, But some of them can be expensive ones. However, little is going to stand in your way while you are in this energetic mood. You will find children very lively. You seem to enjoy taking them out, teaching them various things, and generally bringing out the best in them.

Getting down to your everyday routine will not be the drag it used to be. You can feel a lot of content-ment and happiness in your daily activities. Co-workers will seem so cheerful and pleasant that the days can fly by. Some of you may be taking an interest in healing and alternative therapies.

40th Week/October 1–7

Thursday October 1st. You will be very detached about a relationship. This may be useful if someone wants to discuss a certain matter with you. A brother or sister may need some help with a marital problem. You will enjoy teaching or learning about subjects like computers, driving, or science. A meeting with a counselor or a lawyer should be very productive.

Friday the 2nd. You may have a spirited encounter with a partner this morning. Be careful not to let your aggression lead you into trouble. Try to curb a tendency to be rash and impulsive. You may find that a professional situation gives you a lot of scope for changes and innovations. It may also be a regular little money-spinner. You can enjoy teaching a child special skills.

Saturday the 3rd. Although little is likely to be achieved this weekend, you can get down to some work on corporate and joint accounts. You may want to get out and about and take a look at new property. Being near the sea will especially appeal to you. This will be a good day for therapy work. You can be very intuitive at times, especially about financial situations.

Sunday the 4th. Keep your daily activities simple and peaceful. You may be more sensitive than usual to any undercurrents of atmosphere and moods around you. The day will be rewarding for those involved in healing and medical work. You will tend to feel more deeply about spiritual issues. For some, in fact, this can be a day for some quite mystical experiences.

Monday the 5th. A partner may decide to go on an unexpected journey. You can feel uneasy about a child's education. However, a journey to some beauty spot will go a long way toward transforming your mood. You can really enjoy some intense or emotional music and art. A visit to a museum can be fascinating. You may feel a real desire to buy some new clothes.

Tuesday the 6th. A trip to the seashore with the family can really cheer you and invigorate you. You will enjoy physical activities this morning and feel a need to keep on the go. This will be a favorable time for studying subjects connected with the spiritual or with healing. Later in the day, you may be asked to undertake a special responsibility at work.

Wednesday the 7th. Unexpected occurrences at work can turn out to be quite exciting. A business partner may have some new ideas for a talk or advertising campaign. You can enjoy going to a really different art show or concert together. Dealing with members of the public can have some strange little twists. It isn't easy when people don't observe the rules.

Weekly Summary

You cannot say that dealing with other people is the easiest of your tasks these days. You can find that you get irritable at the least thing. It may be very hard to adapt to a partnership; you may feel like breaking free from other people's odd ways and restrictions. However, a good talk with someone can really clear the air. You certainly cannot say that life is boring.

This can be a good time for getting into some sort of therapy or research work. For some of you, this may involve secret or hidden matters. Psychological and spiritual subjects can be of particular interest. But other Leos may be more interested in healing and medical work. Joint ventures with others can also mean that you make some money or can at least raise the necessary funds. This is not a time to go it alone.

It will be a good week for studying some unusual and intriguing subjects. Some of you will begin to take up astrological work. Students can find it hard going on Monday. A teacher may not be entirely in agreement with your particular approach. You will enjoy a trip immensely this week, perhaps because of some exotic location in the cards.

41st Week/October 8–14

Thursday the 8th. The morning will be a good time for career interests. You can enjoy working with others at your usual activities. In fact, there can be quite a sympathy and bond with co-workers. The evening is likely to be very busy socially. You may enjoy some physical activities such as aerobics or yoga. A group of people can make you feel a little cross.

Friday the 9th. You and a partner can enjoy a group activity. You may meet someone who is quite influential in your local area. You should be able to write or speak very well. This can be very helpful for drama students. A calm approach to a money matter will be the wisest. You will be far more stable and in control of things. You can be the life and soul of a party tonight.

Saturday the 10th. A meeting with a group of youngsters can go very well. You may be taking a group of schoolchildren to some historic place. A private enterprise you have established can keep you very busy. You may decide to take work home and finish it in peace and quiet. Working with elderly folks can be rewarding. Fund-raising activities will be successful.

Sunday the 11th. This will be a quite enjoyable day even though you may want to be left in solitude more than usual. You can relax with a good book, watch romances on the TV, and generally laze about. It may be hard to tell a youngster the facts about someone who is sick, maybe in the hospital. You can spend the day lost in dreams or fantasies. This may be helpful to the artistically inclined.

Monday the 12th. A neighbor may look to you for some support and sympathy. You are likely to be in a benevolent and generous mood. A relative may be asked to resign or get the sack. You will need to be around to help cheer someone up. Deal with finances. You may want to buy someone a present. A youngster may keep you home from work.

Tuesday the 13th. Your personal need to talk things over with a partner can be strong. You may break through a barrier of silence and really change a situation. A telephone or appliance in the home can be out of order, and you may have to call in a repair person to sort things out. A lover can be very intense at times, in the mood for a little passion.

Wednesday the 14th. You need to use your charm and to look very presentable. Meeting a local dignitary can be very exciting. You may have to talk about a child's education with a school principal. Students will need to consult their teachers before making any decisions. Energetic and lively communications will take place with family members.

Weekly Summary

This will be a favorable time for group and social activities. You and a mate are going to enjoy doing things together again. You are sure to shine at gatherings and functions and attract attention. Your conversation will be of interest to some influential people. It will be a good idea to cultivate these new acquaintances. Giving talks, taking seminars, making plans for writing a book or thesis will all do well.

Taking some time off to work alone and have a little bit of solitude can be very refreshing. You may have a lot to do with sick people this week, and this can include visiting hospital patients or seeing people in homes or institutions. You may find that you can stimulate the imaginative faculty a good deal. This may make you a little lazy and apathetic. Or it can be highly motivating to the creative side of your nature. You may find going to art galleries and museums interesting too.

This will be a good time to get going on your own personal projects, dreams, and schemes. You will be very attractive to others right now. People will tend to listen to you and find you fascinating and charming.

42nd Week/October 15–21

Thursday the 15th. You may get very angry at a lover; however, you will be able to keep an air of control, especially when in public together. It can be a very explosive time for family matters. Maybe you are worried about some financial situation. If so, take time to discuss it calmly rather than overreact. A child may have some problems at school.

Friday the 16th. This will be a good day for sitting down and reevaluating certain situations. You can begin to work on personal accounts in detail and learn all your ins and outs. This can be a quiet and uneventful day. You may want to do some shopping for useful items. Take stock of your possessions for insurance purposes and make sure you are well covered.

Saturday the 17th. This will be a good time to get on with healing work. Pets can be very important to you just now. You may decide to buy some fish or other aquatic pet that can soothe your nerves. A partner may have some odd things to tell you. A friend may come to join the family for a bit. You will tend to feel quite resentful toward a lover. Children could be noisy and ill-mannered.

Sunday the 18th. If you can persuade a neighbor to look after a child, you may be able to have a free day. A partnership will seem to be getting too possessive and stifling for your liking. You can really feel the need to break away from a relationship. A friendship can transform your way of thinking. You can benefit from a real heart-to-heart talk with someone.

Monday the 19th. You will be in a far more amiable and relaxed mood. You can feel a great deal of fondness for a kindly neighbor. Travel around the local area. You will enjoy going shopping for beautiful items. Elegant clothes can be high on your list. Enjoy the peace and tranquillity of your own space. Relationships will be more harmonious.

Tuesday the 20th. The morning can be spent with a special neighborhood friend. A principal may have some disappointing news for you about a child. Students may need to be more realistic about a study matter. Maybe you are losing interest in your particular subject. You will tend to feel a bit low later in the day and a little tired. Work seems to be boring just now.

Wednesday the 21st. This can be a good time for a meeting with relatives. You will enjoy discussing the past at a family get-together. Deal with correspondence and bills. A phone call to a brother or sister will be appreciated. Parents may want to talk to you about an emotional issue. You can think deeply about past grievances.

Weekly Summary

Although you may really be in the mood to get out and have some fun, you will have to consider financial matters a little more carefully. This can feel very restricting at times. You will find that this is a week when you do some hard thinking about your values and your ideals. Maybe you wonder just how you can put your savings or capital to better use. Your feelings can be very altruistic and self-sacrificing. An interest in spiritual matters and healing or charity may be part of your new plan.

There could be quite a lot of visiting back and forth with your neighbors this weekend. You may really enjoy meeting and having time to catch up on the news and gossip. You will enjoy a shopping spree. You are inclined to want things that look and feel beautiful. This can be a good weekend for traveling to local places and finding interesting beauty spots that are quite new to you.

If family members have a lot to tell you, give them time to talk it through. There may be a lot of past issues coming up for review. Try not to hold on to old grudges and grievances. This can be a good time for clearing up any old family papers and documents.

43rd Week/October 22–28

Thursday the 22nd. Be sensitive to family undercurrents. You may feel anxious about a pet's health. Don't let neighbors get too annoying about a boundary problem. It will be better to take a broad view of it all and maybe let them have their way. It may be hard to accept an apology from someone who has said unkind things, but you will be wise to forgive and forget.

Friday the 23rd. A mate or spouse can really change things. He or she may have some revolutionary ideas for getting out and having some fun together. You can do with something to liven your spirits just now. Don't let a parent be a killjoy. You're young only once. You may find that a boss has some overtime for you, which can spoil your plans for a night out.

Saturday the 24th. Don't overestimate how much you have to spend. Keep an eye on the details of your current ins and outs. You can get sentimental about something or someone. A neighbor or relative may be in trouble and need some advice and sympathy. You may be worried about the health of the person. An adolescent may need some discipline, but try not to be too unbending.

Sunday the 25th. You can get on in a far more orderly and organized fashion now. You may find that a parent is a lot more understanding and ready to compromise on an issue. If you are dealing with older children, you need to treat them as if they were mature. You may be called into work for some reason and have to give up your Sunday relaxation.

Monday the 26th. Daily activities can keep you very busy. But it may be that you have to make some efforts to earn a bit of extra cash now. You can feel a good deal more cheerful about a certain financial situation. Health matters are promising. Positive steps can be taken to help yourself or others. A pet will be much improved. Co-workers can be full of wisecracks.

Tuesday the 27th. Take things as easy as you can. You may find that a bad back, teeth problems, or irritated nerves can set you back again. You may be attempting to do too much at work. Why take on all the responsibility? There must be others who can help. You will find that talking about the past with a relative releases some painful memories.

Wednesday the 28th. A partner can still surprise you. You may find that a clash with a parent is making problems for you and a mate or spouse. You may need to get the advice of an expert to help with some creative activity or hobby. Those of you who are trying to have a baby will need to see a doctor or specialist. This isn't a good time for you and a lover.

Weekly Summary

This will not be at all an easy week for family matters. You can feel very worried about a teenager or older child's behavior and problems. If you yourself are a youngster struggling to free yourself from home, parental restrictions can be very frustrating just now. This needs to be a time of compromise rather than rigid discipline or mere rebellion. You may be having delays sorting out a property matter.

Although you should be having a good time and may really long to get down to some more creative issues, it seems that various duties and responsibilities will keep getting in the way. This will make you very irritable and frustrated at times. Maybe your plans are too wide and diffuse. You need to work on various inspirations and ideas and get them into shape. It will not be a good time for gamblers and speculators.

You may need to look to health matters after the weekend. Each day you can tend to feel an up and a down. Most of your problem can be due to overload and too many burdens on your shoulders. Naturally, this can make you tense and tired. But try not to get too sorry for yourself. Be practical instead.

44th Week/October 29–November 4

Thursday the 29th. It will not be a good idea to go raking up the past with a mate or spouse. You can be unforgiving about an old grudge. However, relations with a parent will now be a good deal more loving and harmonious. Maybe you can find it easier to see one another's viewpoint. This will be a good day for decorating a home or working in a garden. You can find some peace there.

Friday the 30th. You will feel a lot easier in your mind about a property matter. Money may at last be put down, and things can go ahead. A need to talk to someone about your deeper feelings can take some of you into therapy work. You can be much more at ease with a parental figure. This is likely to be a good day for you, although you still will keep a low profile.

Saturday the 31st. You may consider this a good time to take a few risks and increase your earnings considerably. Take care, however, as you may be deceiving yourself about a particular issue at work. You can find it hard to meet a deadline. Worrying will not help. Just be honest about it. Your health can be poor, and you may be quite tired.

Sunday November 1st. If you can get together with a younger relative, you can have a really deep conversation. Ideas for making some money as a family venture can be fun to work out. Later in the day, you can set off with a determination to enjoy yourself. You may think of some new ways of entertaining the children. Creative work is favored.

Monday the 2nd. This will be a good time for taking a journey and having a change of scenery. Fresh places and sights can be quite energizing and stimulating. You may be steadily working away at your studies. In fact, this can be a time of renewed interest in what you are doing. Talking with others about philosophical and spiritual matters is sure to give some insight into life.

Tuesday the 3rd. You may find a long air journey a bit tiring. This can be a difficult time for getting to grips with mystical or abstruse ideas. However, you may find it even harder to get to grips with everyday reality at times. The afternoon may be very trying when dealing with a partner. You can get into a lively political argument before you go to the polling place.

Wednesday the 4th. A more energetic approach to a professional problem can really help you to get through a heavy schedule. You should be earning a good deal. You will be ambitious to do really well and succeed at something special. Therapy or research work will show progress. You will feel optimistic and more cheerful about a career and financial matter.

Weekly Summary

This may be a good time to get yourself organized on a property or real estate matter. You will find that a parent is very helpful about lending you some cash toward such a project. If you are involved in therapy work, this will be a time when a good deal can be brought up about past issues and childhood problems. This can help you to feel more relaxed and peaceful. An official may be curious about a joint money matter.

If you need to make a trip for business purposes, be sure to get as well organized as you can. You may find some sort of confusion arising over a routine matter. This can be a difficult time for students. You don't seem to be too clear about your work or what you really are aiming for. It will be best just to plod on for the present and wait until things are less hazy. You can feel quite disappointed with a certain spiritual way of life. The reality of strict disciplines may not be to your taste, after all.

Be prepared for some sort of change to take place in your working life. A partner may be restless of late and need to make a break. You seem very optimistic just now about a proposed expansion of your business.

45th Week/November 5–11

Thursday the 5th. You will enjoy some very unusual social gatherings. A theatrical entertainment may be bizarre but fascinating. You can find that a young person is ready to break free and be independent. The day will be good for deep and meaningful conversation with a lover. You are likely to be very detached about it all. This certainly will help when things begin to get too intense.

Friday the 6th. Try to keep calm over an annoying financial problem. You may have been trying to expand too rapidly in all directions. If you have been too optimistic, you are now about to face the facts. A decision about a property matter needs to be carefully considered. Don't let anyone talk you into spending more than you can really afford.

Saturday the 7th. This may turn out to be a very quiet day. You may feel in limbo while waiting for things to start happening. A lover will tend to be very intense and compelling. There may be need to speak out about things that have been held down for a long time. A child can be surprisingly determined to do well with his or her lessons. You will feel creative, but little may get done.

Sunday the 8th. A family reunion can be very enjoyable. You will feel lively and happy. Unexpected news from a relative will really buck you up. You may learn that someone is expecting a child. In fact, for some of you Leos, a new addition to the family may well be here. Just having a little gathering of close friends at your home will make you feel very content.

Monday the 9th. An elderly in-law may need to be admitted to or visited in a home or hospital. You will feel very sympathetic toward someone who is sick. Dealings with children will go well. They can be changed for the better. You are very content to be busy around the house right now. Decorate or make some improvements to home and property.

Tuesday the 10th. Your relationship with a parental figure is likely to be very cheerful and good-natured now. You can feel a lot more understanding of what went wrong before. Now will be a good time to sort out a money matter with someone influential such as a bank manager or accountant. A legal aspect of a property deal may need talking over with a lawyer.

Wednesday the 11th. You will tend to be serious at times, and even quite subdued and thoughtful. Your ambitions are sure to be of importance now and there can be a strong urge to succeed. Students can benefit from this surge of discipline and organization. The day will be good for traveling for professional reasons. You may decide to take up a specialized study to help you with your career aims.

Weekly Summary

There seems to be a lot going on for you socially at the start of this period. You may find that various conversations with a group of people tend to turn a bit hot and steamy. Keep away from political matters if you can. A meeting with a group of friends may not be very enjoyable. Discussions about morbid subjects may make you feel quite tense. You can get angry with a friend who may have let you down over a money matter.

Just getting on with various private activities can be soothing over the weekend. For many of you, there can be all sorts of happy family get-togethers and reunions. This can cheer you up, especially if you have not been well. There may be a lot to do for elderly folks who need some care and assistance now. You can be very caring and self-sacrificing, although it isn't always easy looking after the sick.

The week is likely to end well. You may feel an upsurge of ambition and a rekindling of your own neglected plans and desires. You can decide to take up various courses and activities that further your own interests. Students are especially likely to get down to work and feel a deeper sense of duty and obligation.

46th Week/November 12–18

Thursday the 12th. You will tend to take a firm and immovable stance on a property matter. Others may try to get you to sign a contract against your better judgment. You may decide to make or change a will. Children may need to be completely outfitted with clothes or school supplies. A car can prove costly if it needs repairs and maintenance.

Friday the 13th. Those who feel troubled by the date can relax. This can turn out to be a really fortunate time for money matters. You will be able to enjoy yourself with a family member. Having dinner with a parent or older child can be a lively activity. You may be in a mood for spending on clothes, furnishings, or other beautiful objects for the home.

Saturday the 14th. If you can deal tactfully with a lover or partner, you may be able to settle some controversial issues that have arisen between you. The day will be good for creative activities that involve a group of people. Your interest in a neighbor can be more than being just good friends. You will enjoy local theatricals and pantomimes. Children can have a very good time.

Sunday the 15th. This can be a good time to plan your shopping list and to write your first batch of early Christmas cards. A gossip with a neighbor will be fun. You can enjoy making lots of little trips and social calls around the local area. Work with computers or go for rides in a new car. The afternoon can be very cheerfully spent with family activities.

Monday the 16th. Older people can slow up your pace. However, you will be more than ready to give up time and effort to care for them. Watch your health, as you may feel a trifle stiff and creaky. You can be in a highly philosophical frame of mind. However, something or someone may be proving a disappointment spiritually. You need to be a lot more realistic in more ways than one.

Tuesday the 17th. A change in a family matter may make you feel a bit upset. A partner's crankiness really can get you down at times. However, you seem able to be more forgiving and understanding. You may long to make the home look as perfect as you can. This may mean getting out on a shopping spree and buying expensive items. You may still be involved in redecorating and making it all nice.

Wednesday the 18th. A fresh start in a family matter can be a relief and bring freedom all around. You can really enjoy moving into a larger space. Some of you may be taking up residence in some foreign country or moving a long way off into the country. This will be a propitious day for those who are about to give birth. It can be a very cheerful and optimistic day for you Leo people.

Weekly Summary

Dealing with various financial interests can be a bit of a trial at the start of the week. But you will be quite determined to clear the way and get things moving. You may decide to make a will at some point, or there can be matters to clear up with inheritances and so on. Be very careful when signing any contracts. Meetings to sort out various corporate money matters may turn into regular power struggles.

You can really enjoy your local social life on the weekend. Neighbors will be very pleasant and chatty. You can catch up on all the local news. Being with relatives can also be more fun now. You may feel a lot closer to a brother or sister than you have for a while. Decisions may need to be made between you about a parental figure or a child's future. You can enjoy phone calls, letters, and generally just driving about locally and shopping.

This will be a good time for family activities and interests. You seem to be in the mood to make your home look as nice as possible. This can mean indulging in all sorts of beautiful new items and furnishings. Giving little parties and having folks in for dinner can give you a lot of fun and pleasure.

47th Week/November 19–25

Thursday the 19th. Things will go very smoothly and delightfully. You will be feeling very sociable and cheerful. Harmonious feelings between yourself and a partner will make life a lot easier. Children can be lively and a handful, but you can really enjoy them. Go to the theater and have fun with close friends. You will be very charismatic and attractive these days.

Friday the 20th. You may find that a discussion with a lover can be humorous and fun. But don't get carried away with a business proposal that looks risky. You may be too optimistic about the outcome of a recent speculation. Be wary about any documents you are asked to sign. A publishing matter may not work out quite as you were hoping.

Saturday the 21st. You may fall out with a lover over a silly detail. You will need to keep your temper over an annoying money matter. You may find that getting ready for a trip or journey for a professional reason is a bit exhausting. Students may now be into a last-minute panic with exams and revision. Just keep at it steadily, and all should be well.

Sunday the 22nd. You can take life on a day-to-day basis. This can be a far more relaxing day than yesterday. Dealing with spiritual matters can help you to unwind and feel less anxious. Your compassion and gentleness toward a parent or child is wonderful. This can be a good time for quietly dealing with daily tasks and activities. A spiritual leader can be very helpful.

Monday the 23rd. This is likely to be a very fortunate time. You can really enjoy dealing with small routine matters. A lot can be done if you apply yourself to it energetically. Health interests will be important. A real change can be seen now in a child's attitude. In fact it may seem like a transformation at times. A lover is sure to be passionate and intense. You may feel very possessive about a loved one.

Tuesday the 24th. You will get on well with an important family member. You may have to take the lead in some situation at home this morning. You can really feel your old self and at ease when with your family and at home. The day will be good for outdoor work and other activities. A partner can be keen to help you enjoy yourself socially. A theatrical production will be most enjoyable.

Wednesday the 25th. You will enjoy conversations with others. You may hear from someone who is living some way off. A letter from a lover may really stimulate your romantic nature. You will enjoy doing some different things socially. You are likely to be in a creative mood and can make some unusual and beautiful things. Children may be excitable and energetic.

Weekly Summary

Make good use of all your energies and ideas to get on with some creative interests if you can. You should be able to get others to be enthusiastic too, maybe even help you out financially. Don't promise more than you can deliver. You tend to exaggerate certain skills. This will be a good time for being with children. They can be noisy and lively, but you will be able to keep them well under control.

You appear to gain a lot of pleasure these days from just doing the ordinary, everyday little things. You can enjoy a very spiritual day on Sunday. Caring for those less fortunate can be your way of living up to your ideals. Sick people will need your sympathy; help and healing are sure to find you very sensitive to their needs. This week will be good also for dealing with small animals. Your health will be much improved now. Being by the sea can be therapeutic.

You and a mate or spouse can have a very pleasant time after the weekend. A lot of little journeys together can also be fun, especially if you are on vacation or retired now. Shopping and enjoying art shows, music, and the theater can also be ways of bringing the two of you closer.

48th Week/November 26–December 2

Thursday the 26th. A steady attitude toward a partner is the best this Thanksgiving Day. You may look to others for some support and guidance, or you can be the one to organize them. Later in the day, you may find that a lover is being stubborn about a joint money matter. Relatives are likely to come from quite far away to touch base with friends and the home folks.

Friday the 27th. You can be doing very well with a certain business deal. This can lead to quite a rapid expansion of your present finances. You may find that a creative work is now selling well. Writing music can keep some of you busy. Be realistic about how much extra work you can do on a daily basis. You may be a bit confused about a message you receive.

Saturday the 28th. This can be a pleasant day if it is spent at work. You may receive a lot of help and kindness from a colleague. You can get very angry with a local person. A letter or phone call may be upsetting in some way. Speaking tactfully to a lover can help to sort out a difficulty. A child can be very charming and lovable. You may enjoy writing music, romances, or painting a picture.

Sunday the 29th. Although a partner seems to have changed his or her mind about a journey, you will be relieved. You can enjoy a trip to the theater or a supermarket a good deal more. Spending on books, clothes, and appliances can give you a lot of fun. You may enjoy reading or writing poetry. Creative efforts or relaxing hobbies can be pleasant. You will be at ease with a lover.

Monday the 30th. You will feel calm and steady. Your attitude toward life is philosophical and sensible. A journey for business purposes can be quite boring. The morning can be spent traveling about, but a lot can be achieved. Later you may feel a need to dodge your routine tasks and do something different. A powerful and compelling person you know can sweep you off your feet.

Tuesday December 1st. You may be quite ready for a change to take place in your career now. You can really enjoy the fact that things are rapidly expanding and there is more to do. A partner seems to be taking a lot more initiative about things. Meetings with a boss can bring about some unusual reactions. You will be creative and full of unique ideas.

Wednesday the 2nd. A sympathetic and sensitive partner can make all the difference. You may need to talk someone into making a decision about a child's future. You can be in a mood for sensual and luxurious pleasures. This can prove to be expensive, but who cares? A romantic evening and lively conversation can make this a special day for you and a loved one.

Weekly Summary

Corporate finances and other joint money ventures may come up for review this week. You may need to meet with someone who can help you to get a creative project off the ground and financially more viable. This will not be an easy time to see a bank manager or a lawyer. It doesn't look likely that much will be forthcoming from these sources except bills. It will not be a good time to take a risk, speculate, or gamble your hard-earned cash away.

You may feel a lot more at peace with in-laws these days. If you need to travel this week, you will find that a lover is good company and delightful to be with. You may have some duties or other responsibilities to deal with on a journey. Older people you meet while traveling can be very interesting. An official may help when things go too slowly for your taste on Monday morning.

You seem to be feeling somewhat changeable on a professional matter. If you haven't got all the facts at hand, it will be best to get wised up to what is needed and expected of you. You may feel a bit tired of routine and need to get away from it all. Make some creative changes, do not just throw up the whole thing in a fit of caprice and boredom.

49th Week/December 3–9

Thursday the 3rd. You will find some unusual ways of entertaining yourself and friends. It may be hard to keep your exuberance down at times. You will enjoy going to the theater and may even be performing yourself. Larger-than-life characters will fill the bill nicely. This can be a good time for being with a group of unconventional people.

Friday the 4th. This is likely to be a much steadier day. You seem to have calmed down considerably. The morning will be spent dealing with official matters and clearing up things. You can terminate your association with a group of people. An old friend may get in touch. You can rush about like mad this afternoon. A lot of shopping and other errands may need to be done.

Saturday the 5th. This can be a happy day. You may want to be on your own to sort through various presents, write cards, and generally get lots of little jobs and errands done. You are likely to be in a philanthropic mood. This can mean doing some sort of charity work. Your spiritual interest may incline you to read philosophical books. A warm message from a lover will make you feel good.

Sunday the 6th. You may feel slower and a little tired. Don't try to do too much; just relax and let things be. A trip somewhere can take a long time and be most frustrating or subject to delays. A partner may not be well or may be oversensitive about something you say. You need to be ready to smooth ruffled feathers and feelings.

Monday the 7th. This can turn out to be an interesting day, with interesting encounters. You may find that you have a lot more power over someone than you have realized. But try not to be too controlling. A child may really transform your life. You may feel like a break from certain relationships or a business partnership. Give it careful thought before doing anything too rash.

Tuesday the 8th. You may run into some old buddies from college and have a wonderful party. Or you can meet a loved one and take a trip. You may prefer classical locations and old cities now. Your interests will be serious and high-minded. Your attitude will now be more stable, and others will look to you for comfort and support.

Wednesday the 9th. You may contest a tax bill, a will, or some other financial matter very strongly. This can be a splendid time for settling down for a disciplined stretch of work at a hobby or other creative pursuit. You will tend to be a bit overpowering toward a lover. Try not to mold others to your own ends and needs. Be as flexible as you can.

Weekly Summary

Start the month by getting into the Christmas spirit. You seem to have a busy and varied social calendar. Interesting people to meet, unusual activities and groups to work with can all make this a special time. You are likely to be in a very creative mood. This can lead you to take part in pantomimes, musicals, and other stage productions. You may try to do too much all at once. So take care, or you will soon be knocked out by it all.

You need to take a break and retire from the scene literally for a day or two. In this time, you may need to catch up with various private matters. Some may be business, some personal. You may have a few things to wind up and finish off. Older people may also need to be attended to in some way. You can enjoy being philanthropic and helping out with charity matters.

This is likely to be a very favorable time for you in a highly personal way. You can be full of seductive charm right now. Try not to be too pushy, even though others may be under your spell and ready to do your slightest bidding. You may feel a little unsure and confused about a relationship. Try to keep steady and calm. You aren't really seeing things straight.

50th Week/December 10–16

Thursday the 10th. In some ways this can be a very lucky and favorable time for you financially. It will all depend on how awake you are to various opportunities and leads. You may tend not to see the wood for the trees. Someone influential will be of great assistance to your schemes. You can have a very pleasant time with a lover. A child's good fortune will cheer you up.

Friday the 11th. This will be a good day for lovers but not for those who gamble with money. You may hope for a big win. You may get a little win, but basically this is not yet time for your lottery number to come up. The morning may be spent working out what to charge for your various creative works. You can enjoy buying presents for children and spoiling a loved one in the nicest way.

Saturday the 12th. Neighborhood entertainments can be fun for you and a partner. You can really enjoy yourself making various little journeys. This can be a busy time for salesmen. You may need to travel about a good deal. Selling children's items will do best. You may find that a child has had a wonderful time at a party or a theatrical production.

Sunday the 13th. You can enjoy yourself with a lover. You may feel very creative these days and be busy writing and working on various ideas. You can deal successfully with phone calls, fax machines, and with writing cards and letters. You may be wise to cancel a journey. Delays and other problems can make any sort of travel frustrating. You may feel a bit weary and overloaded at times.

Monday the 14th. This can turn out to be a disjointed and disrupted day in many ways. However, you appear calm and relaxed and take all your daily activities in your stride. You will enjoy cooking and crafts. Preparing for a dinner party may mean enlisting the help of a mate or spouse. Family members can be on harmonious terms with each other for once, especially if they are celebrating Hanukkah together.

Tuesday the 15th. This can be a happy day for a family get-together. You and a partner will be friendly and welcoming to all the clan. There may be a tendency to be quite lavish with your entertainment. Be sure that you don't overwhelm others. Keep things simple and attractive. You may feel very excited and sparkling with wit and humor.

Wednesday the 16th. This will be a good day for those who are in love. You can feel as if you have met your ideal mate. Conversation can flow and feelings can be strong. Children can be adorable acting in Nativity plays. Don't be surprised if you need your box of tissues. Writing activities and general communication are favored. A partner can be very easygoing and gentle. You may enjoy spiritual activities together.

Weekly Summary

Don't be too reckless with any money matters this week. You may be very liberal but also gullible. Buying all sorts of useless objects may turn out to be a great waste of time and cash. Presents will need to be grand to please your idea of generosity. You can certainly enjoy a small wager; you may even do reasonably well from it. But don't expect to hit the jackpot on this occasion. Just look on any gambles and speculative attempts as a bit of Christmas fun.

A lot of rushing about and scurrying hither and thither will be the way this weekend. You may be preparing for various festivities and need to do as much local shopping as you can. The time will be good also for entertaining and being entertained by neighbors. This can be a good time to get know one another, especially if you seldom get a chance to meet at other times of the year. You may have some trials and tribulations while traveling this weekend.

This is always the traditional time for families to get together. You don't intend to prove the exception to this rule. It can be a very happy time for you all and very harmonious. Preparing food and presents will give you a lot of pleasure.

51st Week/December 17–23

Thursday the 17th. This can be a day for racing off to the shops for last-minute presents. You can do very well and get quite a few bargains, finding just the things you were looking for. Deep and intense encounters with a lover are a possibility. You can feel a lot of energy and passion. This may cause at times tension which needs a variety of outlets.

Friday the 18th. A trip can mark a turning point in a professional situation. You may meet an important official who can help you with various creative and artistic schemes. You will feel on top of the world. It may now seem as if a lot more notice is being taken of your efforts and your work. The day will be good for dealings with an influential and mature person.

Saturday the 19th. This is likely to be a quiet and uneventful day. Use a peaceful day like this to catch up on your everyday and ordinary activities. You can now get the house cleaned up and ready for the next round of entertaining. Organize files and sort out correspondence at work so it can be clear for next year. Your health will be good, and you will feel quite relaxed.

Sunday the 20th. Although this can be a very active and busy day, you will continue to feel calm and peaceful. It will be a good day for giving a little party for your colleagues either at home or at work. You can make good use of a recent bonus and go out on the town. Neighborhood activities may require your help and assistance. You will be sure to give generously of time and money.

Monday the 21st. This can be a tough day for travelers. If you are trying to get to see in-laws, you may find that a visit has to be delayed. Or older people may be having health problems and cannot come to visit you. You and a partner will be in good rapport and sympathy with one another. You may even be quite telepathic. Romance will play a major role.

Tuesday the 22nd. A special friend can be great company now. You and a mate or spouse are likely to be very absorbed in each other's company and conversation. You may flare up occasionally over silly trifles. A lover may be wonderful but can also irritate you a good deal. However, keep cool; nothing is worth getting worked up about. You can enjoy cooking with a group of friends.

Wednesday the 23rd. This will be a steady kind of day. You will feel calm and confident when dealing with others. It will be a fine time for those who enjoy being with young people. You will find a group of youngsters ready to work hard at a creative project. Working with the handicapped can be very rewarding. You may find a partner very supportive and reliable.

Weekly Summary

You are quite determined to enjoy yourself these days. This is going to be a special Christmas as far as you are concerned. You can be very lively and gregarious now. Getting ready for parties, dinners, and family fun will take up time and effort. But you will be ready to throw yourself into it all with gusto. Children's interests will be especially important now, whether you are a parent, grandparent, or only a friend.

Use any spare time you have over the weekend to get on with any neglected mundane tasks around the home and office. You can clear up a lot of backlog. Preparing the little details of things you will need for the festive season may mean enlisting the help of friends and partners. There may be a lot of cooking and cleaning up to do. You will be in very good health now, happy and cheerful. But take care not to do too much on Sunday and overtax yourself.

You and your mate can really start to get going on your social rounds. Visiting neighbors, groups of friends, partying, entertaining, will all be part of the scene now. You can feel very stable and happy in one another's company these days. You both share a realistic philosophy of life.

52nd Week/December 24–31

Thursday the 24th. If you have a few last-minute bills to settle, better get them seen to now. You may forget them otherwise. You will expect a lot from some theatrical production, but it may end up a bit of a flop. However, nothing seems likely to mar your self-confidence at this stage. You can enjoy everyday activities most of all now, and children's company too.

Friday the 25th. Merry Christmas! This can be a very peaceful and happy day for you. You will really enjoy being quite ordinary and just being at home with loved ones. Cooking can be a tremendous pleasure for you. You are sure to entertain lavishly and generously. Lots of presents, lots of love and goodwill can make this a day to remember.

Saturday the 26th. If you are going on a vacation or taking a trip to see relatives, you will feel quite excited. Some of you may be going to some exotic and interesting places. You may feel a little worried about leaving a pet behind. Or there may be tasks you would have liked to finish off. Why not relax and put all this behind you? Spiritual activities can occupy many of you now.

Sunday the 27th. This will be a good day for travelers. You can enjoy yourself immensely, especially if you are taking a cruise. Your daily activities can be a real delight. Sharing them with a loved one will make things even more special. You need to watch a tendency to be impatient and impetuous lest you say something you will later regret.

Monday the 28th. Things will tend to slow down a bit. This can give you time to take in the details and study places you visit and people you see. An official may need certain documents this morning. Be sure that all is in order. You can feel a little tired now and want to spend the afternoon out of the public eye. Good company and interesting conversations will make things a bit lighter.

Tuesday the 29th. You can relax again; things seem to have sorted themselves out. You will find that your professional and career prospects are excellent now. A promotion can mean a good deal of extra money for many of you. You can really enjoy being at work these days. Colleagues and staff will be friendly, co-operative, and pleasant to be with.

Wednesday the 30th. You need to be gentle toward a partner. You may be trying to get your own way over a certain matter. A child can present a few problems. But if it's a battle of wills, you are sure to win. Being sympathetic to others can earn you many new friends. You will enjoy a social activity tonight. A charitable or spiritual group can count on your support.

Thursday the 31st. You will end the year on a very cheerful social note. Enjoy yourself with friends and groups of cheerful people tonight and help see out the Old Year in style. Just take care not to go overboard. You can be highly exuberant, and it will be hard work to sober you up again at the end of a day like this. Partners and other relatives seem likely to be there to join in the fun as well.

Weekly Summary

You will really enjoy your Christmas festivities this year. You haven't a lot of money worries just now, which means that you can be as lavish as you like.

Nothing is likely to please the generous Leo heart more. You do like to shower loved ones with gifts, love, and lots of goodies. You can gain a great deal of pleasure from making things look nice, cooking, doing all sorts of little everyday things. In other words, just looking after everyone's welfare and happiness in your own special way will bring you joy.

It looks as if some of you lucky Leo people are off on a trip or winter vacation now. You do love the sunshine and some luxury and fun. Even visiting the in-laws can be more pleasant than expected. You may even get a chance to sit back for a bit and let others look after you. You can enjoy philosophical conversations now, and there seem to be plenty of these.

Although you may have to return to work fairly soon, you may discover that you are in for a promotion or pay raise. Or a bonus may be awaiting you. Various ideas for expanding your concerns and career interests can make you have something positive to look forward to next year.

DAILY FORECASTS:
JULY–DECEMBER 1997

Tuesday July 1st. You may be on the receiving end of a romantic pass from a friend now. But you may find this offensive rather than flattering. Do not be afraid to express your feelings. Cut across any underhand approach with direct communication.

Wednesday the 2nd. If you feel hesitant to become involved in a new venture, talking it over with a friend or associate will help. You will probably realize that your fears are natural. Your relationship with a love partner can be really special at present.

Thursday the 3rd. You may receive an offer or proposition from an unlikely source. Take time to consider what really is involved. This is not a day for rushing anything. Moods are changeable and egos are fragile, especially yours. Confide in a close friend.

Friday the 4th. Your overriding need for at least part of this Independence Day is going to be to keep yourself to yourself. Being in the spotlight is fine as long as you are able to speak your mind. But you are sensitive and touchy. Brash people can set you off.

Saturday the 5th. Discussions about work or routine tasks are likely to take more time than the chore itself. You probably do not want responsibilities now. Getting out to enjoy yourself with a good friend or a partner is a better idea and healthier too.

Sunday the 6th. You really will be feeling in top form in more ways than one. If a social event is lined up, you are likely to shine there. You will be looking good too and leading the lively conversation. But you may not welcome what a partner does or has to say.

Monday the 7th. You excel now in areas where you do not actually have a great deal of experience. This will be a good day for beginning a new project or for taking up a new activity. A friend or partner can irritate you by trying to hog the spotlight. Speak up.

Tuesday the 8th. Having to be the life and soul of the party can be rather tiring when you do not feel up to it. You may have to entertain business clients or keep your end up socially. And it will be a bit of a struggle. Keep in mind the benefits involved in doing so.

Wednesday the 9th. A clandestine discussion with someone of considerable influence is likely to benefit you. This can be in connection with a promotion or your financial circumstances. Either way, you will feel reassured. Later, enjoy a romantic interlude.

Thursday the 10th. An unusual work opportunity may come your way. It may come from a strange source, but it can be lucrative just the same. Follow up any leads you are given, no matter how vague. Tie up loose ends in connection with financial matters.

Friday the 11th. Today's news is mixed. A choice will need to be made in connection with a child. Do not worry about it too much. You cannot really make a wrong decision. However, you may have problems in convincing your partner. Arrive at a compromise.

Saturday the 12th. A decision made now is bound to work out to your advantage. If ever there is a time when you can have exactly what you want, it is now. Partners are backing you all the way. However, there are hidden forces, and all is not as it appears.

Sunday the 13th. Somebody seems to be misleading you in regard to how much work is involved with one particular job. Allow plenty of time to aid a relative or neighbor who has asked for help. There will be a chance to talk at a more intimate level.

Monday the 14th. There can be battles on the domestic scene now. You seem to be the only person who is able to speak your mind and express what you want. But this does not appear to be doing much good. A break away from it all and in good company, even a short drive, will be the best solution.

Tuesday the 15th. This will be an excellent day for an intimate gathering in your home. Sharing secrets can bring you and a group of friends or associates much closer together. You can have a real laugh about work issues with colleagues too. Do not try to take too much of the spotlight. Try to keep a low profile.

Wednesday the 16th. This should be a very romantic day. Your partner is likely to be extra loving and caring. There will be very good rapport between you. If you are single, you may meet somebody new through cultural activities or a guided tour. Any journey made today favors making new friends.

Thursday the 17th. This will be another good day for romance. Togetherness, in general, is going to be really rewarding. You should feel that you are getting to know one particular person on a much more intimate level. You can be putting a fairly new romance on a much more stable and permanent level.

Friday the 18th. Today is bound to be busy at work. And you will most likely have a lot of responsibilities to attend to. However, you are definitely equal to these. Your natural leadership skills will help you in getting work completed. If you are looking for new work, scan the ads and note pertinent data.

Saturday the 19th. A long but necessary journey can be irritating. It will probably be better to travel alone, with plenty of your favorite music, than with a partner or friend who may be quite trying. You need time for yourself. Be especially cautious tonight, as the Full Moon gives rise to deception.

Sunday the 20th. The lingering effects of last night's Full Moon can create deception and opposition early today. You are likely to find that little things go wrong, things having to do with practical matters. And you cannot really neglect them. In fact, it may be neglect in the past that is the reason for this.

Monday the 21st. This will be a good day for joining forces with other people in order to cut your work or other responsibilities in half. However, be careful that you do not end up just getting together and having a good time. That may be enjoyable, but it will mean that you do not achieve what you set out to do.

Tuesday the 22nd. Having to shell out too much money in connection with social events can cause you to worry. It may be a good idea to suggest that you pool your resources with those of others, rather than have to make a hefty contribution on your own. A romantic encounter is intense. Be on your guard.

Wednesday the 23rd. If you owe money that needs to be paid back over a short term, try to clear the debt now. There may be insurance premiums to meet. Do not put them off or get behind with payments. You will kick yourself if something does go wrong and you have jeopardized your claim this way.

Thursday the 24th. A long-distance trip will bring you a lot of pleasure. You may have the opportunity to do something that has so far been only a dream. Romance is in the air if you wish to pursue it. A meeting with a new partner will be exciting. An existing partner has a surprise for you.

Friday the 25th. You may be feeling nervous about taking a big step, and you can be delaying making a decision because of this. Unfortunately, news or information received now will not make this any easier. But a chat with an understanding friend can help. The whole thing will be more fun than you expect.

Saturday the 26th. A lucrative career opportunity can come your way. Somebody of considerable influence is working in your best interests. You are probably flattered by all this attention. You may feel self-conscious, but that does not mean you will say no to the offer. Consider all your options.

Sunday the 27th. A partner may be in strong disagreement with you on what is the best career move. But you must follow your own instincts. This is not to say that you should not compromise at all. Indeed, your relationships are just as important as your livelihood. A chat with a colleague is inspiring

Monday the 28th. You may want to join a social or professional group. But you realize that the financial cost involved is too great now. This does not mean that you have to give up the opportunity forever. If you have a job interview, you will shine. Self-expression, a basic Leo trait, is enhanced now.

Tuesday the 29th. This will be an excellent day for combining friendship with romance. You will probably find that a partner responds well to your suggestions on how to fill your leisure time. If you are currently single, a relationship with an acquaintance may blossom into something loving and intimate.

Wednesday the 30th. This will be a quiet day on the whole. You are not really in the mood for stepping into the spotlight and being the life and soul of the party. What you need is time to consider where you have been and where you are going. Fortunately, there should be little pressure to distract you.

Thursday the 31st. This will be another day when you will find yourself with plenty of time on your hands, so you can take things at your own pace. Work matters need careful deliberation. You can get a lot of pleasure from spending money on something that is not necessarily essential. Pamper yourself a little.

Friday August 1st. You need time to plan your moves. But more responsibility means that you will not have the opportunity to take things at your leisure. A flurry of new information can throw you off course. Try to deal with the important priorities first.

Saturday the 2nd. Plenty of romantic attention is likely to come your way. You have no shortage of admirers. This will be an excellent time for going to a house or dinner party. In true Leo style, you will attract powerful and provocative partners.

Sunday the 3rd. It is a day for making far-reaching decisions. You are aware of what you really want, which is not always the case. Just the same, a few nagging doubts may be lurking at the back of your mind. Express them to a confidante.

Monday the 4th. You need to go easy with money but without being stingy. One social event may have to be cut out of your schedule because, all in all, it is just going to end up being too expensive. But there are other things you can afford and will enjoy.

Tuesday the 5th. You are bound to be on the go now. It is a good day for financial discussions. A helpful investment or savings scheme can be on offer. You may have to go through a series of negotiations to settle a salary problem. But it's worth it.

Wednesday the 6th. Your main money concern is probably how to earn more or how to increase your current income without too much effort. As there is no such thing as a free lunch, it is likely that you will have to exert yourself more to win the rewards.

Thursday the 7th. You may feel in the mood to plan and throw a house party or dinner party. Partners will back you all the way. If you are single, there can be a lovely offer from someone who admires you. News about children will be very encouraging.

Friday the 8th. Developments in financial matters will be reassuring. You may receive a new job offer or a raise in pay. Other people's generosity may bowl you over. But you are viewed as being deserving of what is coming your way. The only fly in the ointment is that you are trying to run before you can walk.

Saturday the 9th. Cutting comments can really upset you at present. You can find yourself saying something less than helpful in retaliation. But the thing is, you are hurt. And why should you not express your displeasure? Work plays on your mind at a time when you should be resting. Try to switch off.

Sunday the 10th. Domestic scenes can be ugly and difficult. If you live with a partner, you may find that you really get on each other's nerves. You both need more space, and you will be better off pursuing separate social activities. What appears to be a lucrative venture may actually involve hefty financial input.

Monday the 11th. You may feel that your domestic environment is getting you down. The walls seem to be closing in, and you do not have room to breathe. This can lead you to consider a move. Maybe the problem is temporary. But the promise of more money can tempt you into a different setup.

Tuesday the 12th. A romantic encounter can be intense. If you feel unsure about getting involved with somebody new, take your time. Otherwise you will be in over your head before you know it and make yourself vulnerable to being hurt. In an ongoing relationship, expect pleasant surprises.

Wednesday the 13th. Activities designed to keep children happy may turn out to be quite costly. You may squabble over whether or not a certain toy is bought. You have to be firm, but you probably will feel stingy. Try to make it up to them in some other way. Creative endeavors with your partner should be rewarding.

Thursday the 14th. Your working life is busy, but you can complete one project which has been hanging around your neck. If you are attending an interview, you are likely to get the job. Make sure that the terms and conditions are made clear to you. You are about to pull off a stunning coup.

Friday the 15th. Future moves demand making thorough plans, whether they have to do with home or professional life. There can be discussion of a salary increase. This will give you added impetus. If you have neglected your creative side, later hours are ideal for resuming a hobby or artistic project.

Saturday the 16th. Strange, unaccountable problems may develop with your domestic appliances at home. It will probably be best to get an expert in to look at the affected item. But you may find that the problem just disappears in the meantime. You can turn your talents to lucrative ends if you feel industrious.

Sunday the 17th. This will be a good day for spending time with your partner. You may want to sit back and relax together. Or you may be in the mood for more spirited activity. A trip will be a lot of fun, even if the purpose is serious. A gathering with a spiritual theme should be enjoyable.

Monday the 18th. Disagreements may arise with your partner or with a close friend. You do not see eye-to-eye on basic issues. Some compromise will be necessary if you are to improve the situation. If you are single, this will not be your best time for meeting someone new. Socially, go out just for fun.

Tuesday the 19th. This will be a difficult day for financial negotiations. It is likely that you will be talked into something you do not really agree with. Avoid making solid commitments now. It will be better to have time to think things through than to put your signature to anything. Read the small print.

Wednesday the 20th. Extra efforts put in at work now are likely to pay off in a number of ways, although you may not experience the benefits of this until later on. It is important to have a degree of faith and trust in life. This is a good day for beginning a new sport or hobby. It could lead to a new career.

Thursday the 21st. You may be feeling doubtful of your own capacity to cope with certain responsibilities, particularly if it is up to you to get the ball rolling on a new project. But do not be so pessimistic. Good organization is the key to your success. Be patient and take your time to plan carefully.

Friday the 22nd. You may become very confused over the details and minutiae of a current venture. Try not to get too bogged down with trivia. While your plans are subject to fluctuation, you will do best to go with the flow. Not everything has to be completely mapped out in order for things to go well.

Saturday the 23rd. A very lucrative career opportunity can come your way. It will become obvious to you that certain people really value your skills and abilities. Probably the only person who is not entirely convinced of your worth is you. See that a partner does not steal your limelight. You deserve to be in it.

Sunday the 24th. Surprisingly good work opportunities can come your way. The offer of increased responsibility may be exactly what you need. But once again, do not start doubting yourself. If others believe in you, why not you? Some friends may not be supportive, but others wish for your good fortune.

Monday the 25th. You probably are wondering what one associate is trying to achieve with his or her current attitude. You may be called upon to lend money, although you may never see it again. It may be more helpful to discuss the root of the problem than to go along blindly with what is asked of you.

Tuesday the 26th. An acquaintance can help you to overcome your fears about a course of action you are intending to take. This means that you will be able to press forward with conviction and renewed optimism. One of your friendships will move onto a more stable level now. Old problems will be resolved.

Wednesday the 27th. This will be a good day for getting involved in behind-the-scenes activities. You may discover one or two very useful things, especially if you are carrying out specific research. You need more time to yourself than usual now in order to collect your thoughts and do some financial planning.

Thursday the 28th. Other people may pressure you to get out and socialize when you would rather stay at home. If you are feeling in need of a rest, not all the enthusiasm in the world will change your mind. And besides, you should respect it if your batteries are run down and need charging. Be kind to yourself.

Friday the 29th. Routine tasks are likely to be difficult to complete. This can be due to your not having at hand all the facts, information, or documents that you require. Having to chase around after all of these can be very stressful. Aim to take this evening easy, as you probably do need to have a good rest.

Saturday the 30th. You should now be feeling in better form than you have for a while. However, practical tasks may need doing around the home. You would probably prefer to pursue your own private interests. Yet it will not do to neglect what makes your life run smoothly. Bear in mind that partners can be demanding.

Sunday the 31st. This will be a much better day than yesterday for pursuing personal goals. You can take a brave new step in a fresh direction. Adventurous sports activities may appeal to you. Although you are in the mood for taking risks, you will be wise to protect your personal safety. You are likely to pick up a bargain if you go shopping.

Monday September 1st. This holiday will be good for hunting bargains. But you must be discriminating, or you will buy something that ends up in the trash sooner or later. Salespeople are persuasive. You will have to be strong-minded to resist. You can get word of a forthcoming bonus on an investment plan.

Tuesday the 2nd. Money matters are likely to dominate your thoughts. This will be an excellent day for focusing on ways to improve your income. The opportunity may arise for you to put a hobby or talent to lucrative use. Lack of contact from a beau can be disappointing. But do not brood over it.

Wednesday the 3rd. A good career opportunity is likely to come your way now. But not all of the details are being made clear to you, as the whole thing is a bit embryonic. But there is no need to be cynical. This can develop into something productive and sound in time. News from a loved one will excite you.

Thursday the 4th. A partner is very affectionate, making a very generous gesture. A special candlelit dinner for two can be on the agenda this evening. Even if you are not feeling especially amorous, you probably will be by the time the evening is through. If you are going on a date, you are in for a treat.

Friday the 5th. You probably feel like settling down to a good book or else visiting friends you have not seen in a while. It is unlikely that you will get the chance to do the former if you are buried under paperwork. With friends, you may end up having arguments, but a change of scene will be good for you.

Saturday the 6th. A hobby that you usually spend time on at home can turn out to be very lucrative now. But you may feel that this is something you want to keep strictly as a personal interest. A cozy evening spent curled up with your partner should be very satisfying. If you are single, you may meet someone new.

Sunday the 7th. There may be a tense atmosphere at home just now. But you can cut through this by suggesting something that will get everyone out of the house or apartment. Be careful, however, that you do not end up spending more money than you have budgeted for on social activities.

Monday the 8th. This will be a good day for setting your mind to completing routine tasks. You will feel a great sense of satisfaction if you do manage to get one big job out of the way, whether at home or at work. Should you need help with tasks around the home, turn to family or household members.

Tuesday the 9th. You will be in a party mood. But this will be another time when your social life can end up costing you more money than you anticipate spending. Nonetheless, you should have a very good time. Partners can be pushy. You will have to fight to get your own way. A battle of wits will not amuse you.

Wednesday the 10th. You should receive a very nice communication from somebody you are fond of. This may be a love letter from an admirer, or perhaps a loving telephone call from a partner. Those of you who are single may be asked out on dates. New admirers are extremely attractive in one way or another.

Thursday the 11th. This will be a very busy time for you. But you will not find that you have too much on your hands, plus the fact that you are able to make very good progress with whatever you undertake to do. Colleagues at work are helpful and cooperative. You can probably delegate extra work.

Friday the 12th. There can be confusion about the way that routine tasks have to be carried out or about which is the most important priority. If all is not completely clear, it will be best to ask twice in order to avoid costly misunderstandings. Having to travel a long way may sap your time. Try not to panic.

Saturday the 13th. You feel tense and excitable. Everyone around you seems to be buzzing with nervous energy. You have to be careful that you do not end up doing something outrageous. There is a possibility that you will go to extremes at a social function. Keep an eye on how much alcohol you drink.

Sunday the 14th. It is an excellent time for going on some kind of adventure trip with your loved one. This will also work out well with someone you are just getting to know. This ought to be a day to remember in a very positive light. Avoid staying at home if you can. You will probably become bored and irritable.

Monday the 15th. You can stabilize a financial situation in some way now. If you are waiting for news of an alimony settlement, this can come through. It is important that you not be talked out of the sum you previously had in mind. Stand your ground. A clever lawyer will try to change your mind.

Tuesday the 16th. This will be another good day for financial dealings. Something should be settled in your favor. Be sure that all the information is being made available to you, though. Somebody can purposely be leaving out a few vital details. You need to keep an eye on your expenditures when shopping.

Wednesday the 17th. It is going to be productive for you to drop whatever is at present keeping you busy in favor of a change of scene. Obviously, you cannot neglect really vital responsibilities. But you may be able to find ways of dealing with them without actually having to watch over the proceedings. Time spent with a partner will fill you with happiness.

Thursday the 18th. You may feel tempted to do what you did yesterday, and get away from it all. But this will not be so easy. Work responsibilities or other duties may keep you pinned to one place. Rather than feel hemmed in, try to get these factors out of the way.

Friday the 19th. You will probably be assigned an interesting responsibility. This may involve looking after a budget. No doubt, somebody in authority feels confident about placing a lot of trust in you. But you may feel slightly intimidated by this. Try not to. You are the right person for the job.

Saturday the 20th. You may experience a conflict of priorities just now. You probably feel that there are important meetings to attend and events to go to. But practical problems may keep you stuck at home. Do not worry. The fact that you are not on the scene does not mean people will forget you.

Sunday the 21st. There may be tension in a friendship now. This can be because one or the other of you is hoping for more romantic involvement. But if the situation has always been platonic, this may come as quite a surprise to the other person. Whichever side of the coin you are on, try not to rush into anything you will end up regretting.

Monday the 22nd. This will be a much better day for friendships than yesterday. If one relationship seems to have gone off the rails, you can put it all back in order. Thankfully, errors can be corrected now. You may end up having arguments with a partner. Try to be reasonable; it will be in your best interests.

Tuesday the 23rd. What you really need from time to time is a chance to hide away and escape from phone callers or visitors. But luck will have it otherwise. People make a point of contacting you. And, finally, curiosity gets the better of you.

Wednesday the 24th. You will have a chance to concentrate on behind-the-scenes activities without being bothered. Something communicated to you in confidence will make you feel reassured. Money matters are looking promising. However, a boss may fall down on his or her agreement. Talk about it.

Thursday the 25th. The day is likely to be difficult simply because you are having to spend on work or routine tasks more time than you really want to. You will be in a dreamy frame of mind. And there may be emotional factors cutting in on your thinking. Try not to put yourself under a lot of pressure.

Friday the 26th. It would be an exaggeration to say that all your dreams will come true now. But one of them may, as long as a partner does not stand in your way. In fact, if you play your cards right, you may be able to get him or her to help you. There is encouraging contact from a loved one or admirer.

Saturday the 27th. You will be able to have everything just about your own way at present. Socially, you will be in top form. You will shine at a house party and live up to your life and soul reputation. A partner is likely to be the harbinger of good news. There is excitement in your love life now.

Sunday the 28th. Today keep an eye on your possessions as well as on your spending. If you are planning to go out, be sure to lock up all around the place at home. If you are going to a night club, pay the extra fee to store any of your valuables in a safe place. You will then be able to relax and enjoy yourself.

Monday the 29th. You will feel that one special relationship is moving to a more stable level. But do not panic. This does not mean that it is about to become boring. What it does mean is that you should start to feel a lot more secure inside yourself. There is a chance you can consolidate financial gains now.

Tuesday the 30th. Negotiations over money will leave you in a stronger position. Sometimes there is nothing like being well informed to make you feel more powerful. Developments at work should be very encouraging. You really are on the edge of making a dream come true. Look for bargains when you shop.

Wednesday October 1st. There will be mixed news, but most of it is going to be good. You will feel as though you are starting out along a new road with either neighbors or relatives. Your relationships will improve. And there is the chance to get to know new people. Express yourself in a positive way.

Thursday the 2nd. This should be a fairly lively but not strenuous day. It will be a good time for getting in touch with various associates, and especially with people you have not seen in a while. Catch up on your correspondence. Rosh Hashanah celebrations will prod some Leos into turning over a new leaf.

Friday the 3rd. You may start to feel a bit insecure in a relationship now, due to the actions of the other person. He or she is asserting independence. As you need your own as well, perhaps you should not resent this. But talk things over and not just let them ride. You should be able to create compromises.

Saturday the 4th. Your domestic affairs may seem a bit stifling. Get out of your home for a break. Partners can be demanding, which you can do without. Time spent with a child will be very rewarding, especially if you are the provider of a special treat. The youngster will think the world of you.

Sunday the 5th. This is a good time for giving a dinner party or for entertaining at lunchtime. You may feel the need to get together with work associates on a less formal basis. This can provide you with the chance to get to know them on a more intimate level. A partner will bring a lot of excitement into your life.

Monday the 6th. Your romantic prospects look very good now. If you are single, this is a time when you may receive an interesting and appealing proposal. Time spent with either a new or existing partner is likely to be full of laughs and joviality. Let your hair down and really enjoy yourself.

Tuesday the 7th. This is a day for indulging your creative impulses. If cultural pursuits appeal to you, and you have some time on your hands, do pursue them. A visit to an art gallery or movie house can really inspire you. Your romantic life should be fun, although there may not be any significant developments.

Wednesday the 8th. Aim to get your teeth into routine chores, either at home or at work. You will feel the most satisfied with basic issues out of the way. Attention to detail is going to be vital, especially if there are important documents to sign. Do not try to cut corners. It will probably work against you if you do.

Thursday the 9th. Mixed messages at work may be a problem. You need to get to the source of one piece of information so that you can discover what is really going on. If you are on an interview, ask for information that is not freely given to you. Otherwise you will come out feeling misinformed or uncertain.

Friday the 10th. Partners can be unpredictable, both in business and in personal relationships. This can be absolutely infuriating if you are relying on others. However, they may have their reasons. Consider if your expectations are too high or if you are being let down. For some Leos, travel is highlighted.

Saturday the 11th. You should find that partners are much more supportive now and should be an inspiration to you. This will be an excellent time for escaping out of your usual environment with someone whose company you enjoy a lot. It will be good to cut off from work and other responsibilities.

Sunday the 12th. Money matters can worry you. If you have forgotten to pay an insurance premium, get this fixed as soon as you can. Keep valuables safe when in public places. Those who steal have their reasons, but you do not want to be the victim of a theft. It is better to be safe than sorry.

Monday the 13th. This will be a good time for settling accounts that are due or even overdue. Do not allow debts to build up if you can help it. This will also be a good time for clearing out around the home or office. Then you will be ready to begin a new project.

Tuesday the 14th. You may find that you get the opportunity to travel somewhere new and refreshing. There is plenty of creative inspiration in your life. If you are single, you may link up with someone special through educational activities.

Wednesday the 15th. This is another promising day for new opportunities to arise. But there are strings attached. Perhaps you will not have as much freedom to do your own thing. The change of environment that travel brings will still be refreshing.

Thursday the 16th. You have to be wary of taking on other people's personal responsibilities. You may suddenly realize that you are being called on to act well beyond the call of duty with one person. Put your foot down with a partner. Do not become just a prop.

Friday the 17th. You may be accused of being mean or unreasonable. Do not worry. You are trying to get partners or colleagues to handle their own affairs. There are some things you simply cannot do on behalf of other people. Know where to draw the line.

Saturday the 18th. Now you can feel that any responsibility foisted upon you is from choice. See to neglected tasks. Catch up on paperwork and correspondence. Friends may invite you to a social event, but you may not feel like going. You are not obliged.

Sunday the 19th. This is a good day for your partner and friends to participate in mutual activities. Everyone will get along well together. Those of you who are single may be introduced to somebody new by friends. Accept an invitation.

Monday the 20th. A telephone call or letter from an old friend or work associate will be pleasing. This will also be a favorable time for you to be in touch with various acquaintances, both old and new. Something you have set your heart on looks as though it can be realized now. You feel quite optimistic.

Tuesday the 21st. If you feel a bit down, it is probably because you need a change of scene. One particular environment may hold too many painful memories. Escapism helps to clear out any emotional distress that is distracting you from your work. Getting onto open land can release creative energy.

Wednesday the 22nd. You are likely now to want to hide yourself away and pursue work quietly. However, you are also likely to be very much in demand. You may have a more active role to play in decision making than you expect. It is important to attend meetings even if you really do not feel like it.

Thursday the 23rd. You now feel more confident and back to your normal self. This will be an excellent day for creative work. Your energy is no longer blocked. And you have some really good ideas. Partners or work colleagues can be obstructive. Do not let them keep you from the limelight.

Friday the 24th. There should be opportunity to expand your horizons now. You have plenty of enthusiasm for trying something new. This can be a very romantic day for you Leo people, whether you are already attached or not. If you are single, a musical event may bring you into contact with a new love.

Saturday the 25th. You may find a way to consolidate your earnings now, which will turn out to be very profitable in the long run. It is certainly a good time for investing in savings schemes. Restrain your spending on social activities even if you sense the potential for increased wealth in your life.

Sunday the 26th. This will be another good day for planning financial negotiations. Just talking things over with a knowledgeable associate will be a help. An exciting social invitation can come your way. Although you may have mixed feelings, you will probably enjoy yourself if a friend goes with you.

Monday the 27th. It is a good day to seek new employment. You can stumble upon an excellent and lucrative opportunity. If you are currently working, there may be an unexpected chance to earn extra cash. Contact from a loved one will warm your heart. Be in touch with someone you are fond of.

Tuesday the 28th. If there is somebody for whom you are carrying a torch, this is the ideal day to reach out and communicate. You should receive an encouraging response. Partners are open and responsive, so discuss your mutual future plans. This is a chance to tie up vacation and other travel plans.

Wednesday the 29th. On this busy day you may be rushing around, making trips to pick up items that you need at work or for social events. You may get stuck in heavy traffic, which is likely to be frustrating. However, you will have plenty of energy and creative ideas to help you along the way.

Thursday the 30th. People urge you to act swiftly today. But do not make too many snap decisions. Some of the information you are being given is likely to be misleading or incorrect. It will pay to double-check facts. Take your time if you are being urged to put your signature on anything important.

Friday the 31st. This will be a day for tying up loose ends and trying to finish current projects. If you are hoping to conclude a real estate contract, there may be a small delay or problems getting the money together. Be patient. The basic signs are good and little will be lost.

Saturday November 1st. You will be feeling more optimistic and reassured about a residential move. Details still need to be tied up, but you have no reason to doubt that things will go through as planned. This a good time for having a housecleaning. You may unearth something you have missed.

Sunday the 2nd. What a wonderful day for romance! Whether you are in a long-term, ongoing relationship or footloose and fancy-free, togetherness is a real theme for you now. Travel, a film or theater or music event, or restaurant can bring the romance into your life. Single Leos may jump into a commitment.

Monday the 3rd. This can be a day for spoiling the children a little. They may need your help with homework, and they may just appreciate your company as a playmate. This you will probably enjoy, as you are in a frivolous mood. At work, the atmosphere should be sociable and colleagues should be charming.

Tuesday the 4th. A connection you made a while ago with a business associate is likely to turn out to be useful now. Somebody is going to come up with a good idea on how to make more lucrative use of a hobby. This evening will be ideal for dinner for two in a romantic setting, whether at home or in a restaurant.

Wednesday the 5th. You can complete one task at work that has been a bind. Then you will be free to move on to something new. If you have a job interview, you are likely to come out very pleased with yourself. There may be second interviews to face, but you will have made a good first impression.

Thursday the 6th. This will be a good day for seeking clarification on matters that you have put on the back burner. A partner may be acting a little aloof, but you probably know the signs by now. He or she needs time alone. A romantic gesture will be made sooner or later. A fun surprise is being planned for you.

Friday the 7th. Partners are great fun now. At work, the jovial atmosphere makes it easier to get through dull tasks. A legal matter will be settled in your favor. If you are single, you may get to know someone better through shared educational interest. A night on the town may lead to new romance. Be discriminating. Sometimes glamour is only skin-deep.

Saturday the 8th. You will have a passionate time with your lover now. If you are currently unattached, you will meet someone attractive in sports activities or pursuing a hobby. Be careful of your spending, especially if you owe anyone money.

Sunday the 9th. This will be a good day to settle up your accounts and to pay back any money you have borrowed from friends for a short term. You may develop a deeper interest in mystical or occult matters. A tarot reading at a friend's house can be very interesting. You come away feeling reassured.

Monday the 10th. This is another day when you are urged to delve into occult matters in depth and detail. It may be thoughts or discussions about reincarnation and past-life regression that spark your interest. If you decide to look into this practice, choose a practitioner who comes recommended.

Tuesday the 11th. All should go well on a long-distance journey planned for now. However, do anticipate that there can be delays along your chosen route. If you are taking educational examinations at this time, luck will be with you. You may almost think a paper has been designed especially for you.

Wednesday the 12th. Now you want to expand your interests and broaden your horizons. But you may not have much chance to allow your imagination to run riot on what you can do. Work and routine matters are bound to require a lot of concentration. Put some time aside this evening for your own pursuits.

Thursday the 13th. Career prospects soar. You may be offered a position with increased responsibilities. What may go hand-in-hand with this is a formal promotion and raise in pay. If you are temporarily out of work, you have every reason to feel optimistic. The right position is about to manifest itself.

Friday the 14th. You may wonder now if you are ever going to get anything finished. It seems that too many responsibilities are piled on you at once, and you have to rely on other people a lot. Try not to panic. What really needs to happen will happen. If you get behind now, you will be able to catch up soon.

Saturday the 15th. Romantic matters are tricky. You may quarrel with a loved one. This fight might not be forgotten in a hurry. If jealousy is the issue, consider making a compromise. If you are single, you may be plagued in a social setting by someone you do not warm to. Be rude if you have to.

Sunday the 16th. This will be a favorable day for getting together with like-minded friends. It can be reassuring to discuss difficult recent encounters and discover that you have been correct in your actions and responses. Do all you can to fulfill a personal aim, even if you feel it is just a whim.

Monday the 17th. You really need time to think out your plans, but you probably are not going to get it. There will most likely be a lot of practical tasks to attend to. You may end up creating more work if you go racing ahead without considering what you really need to achieve. Try to slow down the frenetic pace.

Tuesday the 18th. You should have much more chance to take life easy now. You probably need a rest. Amble through behind-the-scenes matters at work rather than rush around starting anything new. This is a good time for sorting out paperwork and generally for picking up the pieces after a stressful time.

Wednesday the 19th. The day favors beginning a creative project or endeavor. Children will probably want lots of attention and you are not reluctant to give it. A friend or partner may be jealous and accuse you of being selfish or childish. Perhaps he or she is finding it hard to enjoy life.

Thursday the 20th. You may have problems similar to those of yesterday with partners or friends. They may want somewhat more of your time than you are willing to give. If you find someone too demanding, it will help to speak out. Everyone needs to do their own thing once in a while.

Friday the 21st. Property negotiations can impinge on your time quite a lot. Nevertheless, it will be worthwhile to do all you can to move things along. If a family member needs support, do try to give it, but not to the extent that you have to cast your own needs to the wind. You would probably resent that.

Saturday the 22nd. You may decide that a social event is going to be too expensive for you. However, a little extra work that comes your way can save the day as far as money goes. A romantic interlude may be flattering, but it is possible that you will be the one who has to foot the bill in one way or another.

Sunday the 23rd. You may waste time on the phone, chatting with friends and loved ones. It is good to catch up on everyone's news, but take a moment to consider the bill you may be running up in the process. A chance meeting with someone you like will be fun, but it may take up more time than you anticipate.

Monday the 24th. If there is something on your mind communicate it to a partner or friend. There should be excellent rapport between you. And you can discuss even the most difficult matters with ease. Children need your guidance. Give them plenty of chance to talk about feelings.

Tuesday the 25th. A misunderstanding among colleagues can be the cause of quite a heated debate. You may not feel you want to get too involved, but you can be a good arbitrator. Do not rush job applications. It is going to be better to fill forms out properly and create a good impression if you take your time.

Wednesday the 26th. There are likely to be miscommunications and mixed messages at work. Doublecheck details carefully. You can wind up calling the wrong client if you are not careful. If you are going for an interview, you will probably have to do a lot of pumping the interviewer for information.

Thursday the 27th. The way that a partner acts on this holiday can make you feel that the relationship is no longer on a stable footing. Even if this is true, the real issue is your own sense of personal security. You may be tempted to call an ex, partly for comfort, partly to boost your flagging self-esteem.

Friday the 28th. If you are planning a move to another home, this is a day when final contracts can be tied up. News received now will be reassuring. Make an effort to keep your home tidy. The more ordered your environment, the more organized you will feel.

Saturday the 29th. There should be a great party atmosphere around, wherever you choose to socialize. If you are single, you are likely to meet somebody very interesting at a sports event or dinner party. This person is likely to have hidden depths. This will be a good day for taking the children out somewhere for a surprise treat. Your partner will be very loving.

Sunday the 30th. A trip undertaken purely for pleasure will turn out very well. It will be good for you to get out of your usual environment. You may shop until you drop, but your purchases will satisfy. Your partner is in a romantic mood. Indulge yourselves. If you are single, accept an invitation.

Monday December 1st. This is likely to be a busy and active day for you. The knowledge that it has now turned December may make you want to rush out and get all your Christmas shopping done. But at work you will probably be tied up. It is vital to make certain follow-up telephone calls or brief visits.

Tuesday the 2nd. You probably are going to be even more on the go than you were yesterday. It can be difficult getting things done at work because colleagues will not be very cooperative. It will be better to aim at diplomacy than to lose your temper. Negotiate your way through. You may need to cancel a trip.

Wednesday the 3rd. This will be an excellent day for getting in touch with and seeing friends. If you have no social plans and are invited to an impromptu group event, do go. Try to get clarified some agreements that seemed vague when they were originally made. It may help to request that these be put in writing.

Thursday the 4th. Partnerships should be rewarding. It will be a good day for talking over deep and difficult matters. If you are currently single, there is a good chance of meeting someone you like at a party. Sports activities also will provide opportunities to link up with somebody new. A trip away from your usual surroundings will be pleasurable.

Friday the 5th. Relationships are on a very even keel now. If you have time to spare, aim to spend it with your loved one. Togetherness is special to you. If you are single and do not feel like meeting new people, get together with an old friend.

Saturday the 6th. Money matters can worry you. You may receive a bill that is higher than you expect. Spending related to social affairs may have built up a lot. Pay accounts in part if you cannot do so in full rather than not pay anything at all. Consider ways to economize.

Sunday the 7th. You will be feeling better about money matters than you did yesterday. This is likely to have to do with getting better organized. If you total up your anticipated expenses, you may find that you are better off than you realize. Or you will see where you can save money by cutting back.

Monday the 8th. If you are currently involved in legal proceedings, there can be difficulties at present. You may be questioned in a great deal of detail and will worry that you may be saying the wrong thing. Say nothing until you have spoken with your lawyer. A pleasure trip can provide a welcome break.

Tuesday the 9th. If you have received an invitation to a house party or dinner party at some distance from home and you are thinking that it may be too far to go, go along just the same. You would probably regret not doing so. A last-minute rush with work matters may hold you up. Keep your host informed.

Wednesday the 10th. Mammoth responsibilities may be placed on your shoulders. But there is nothing to worry about; you will sail through them all with minimum effort. The only fly in the ointment will be a partner who complains because he or she feels neglected. Promise to make it up to him or her.

Thursday the 11th. You may experience something of a power struggle in your relationship with a close friend or partner. He or she does not seem to understand that professional matters have to come first at the moment. It may actually help if you are able to involve him or her in your work.

Friday the 12th. A friendship can become strained. This may have to do with your both disagreeing on the best social activities for you to share. There may also be romantic tension between you. Things will be easier if you can pluck up the courage to be totally honest about the way you feel. Clear the air.

Saturday the 13th. This weekend is excellent for going on a trip or adventure activity with a group of friends. Shared educational pursuits will also bring you a lot of pleasure. You need to be able to cut yourself off from everyday matters now. A change of environment will be as good as a rest. This will not be your best day for romance; friendship will be more satisfying.

Sunday the 14th. A friend who persists in pursuing you romantically is making a big mistake. If the message has not gotten through to him or her by now, there is little you can do but be firm and direct. Do not panic if you make a bad start on a new hobby. It may take you some time to become fully conversant with it.

Monday the 15th. This is a day when you will probably feel like running away from it all. You actually may be given the chance to travel. But a long trip may be tiring especially if it is for business reasons. What you really need is a long rest.

Tuesday the 16th. At work, it will be difficult to get your priorities in order. It is also going to be hard to concentrate because your mind will be on other things. If you can delegate some responsibilities, so much the better. Take good care of yourself this evening, when you will need to relax.

Wednesday the 17th. You are eager to pursue personal plans. But it may be hard to do your own thing because your partner objects. Try to find a middle path rather than include or exclude him or her. Breaking away from your usual surroundings will help to clear your thoughts and refresh you.

Thursday the 18th. Partners can be quite selfish and demand a lot from you. You must be firm about sticking to arrangements. It is really not fair if you are being taken advantage of. You may actually have a better time at a dinner party if you attend on your own. If single, you can meet someone charming.

Friday the 19th. You may be panicking if you have waited to do your holiday shopping till now. And you may be wondering if you have enough money to buy any gifts at all. Sit down and work out what is feasible. Remember that small gifts can be just as pleasing as the more expensive ones.

Saturday the 20th. Social activities are likely to be costly at the moment. You may feel that you need to cancel just so that you will be able to afford the big day itself. But do not be hard on yourself. Have some fun. If your children are difficult, it is probably caused by the excitement of the season.

Sunday the 21st. If you are purchasing foods and other essential items for the holiday, you may be irritated at how expensive it all turns out to be. Remember, it is only once a year. News may cause you anxiety, but do not jump to conclusions. You may have only half the facts now. There is more to come.

Monday the 22nd. Confer with your partner before you make any major moves. Do not undertake a long trip without planning it well first. You can find yourself stuck in traffic for hours. Avoid going along what you know to be the busiest routes unless you absolutely have to because of the store you need to visit.

Tuesday the 23rd. All the things that you have been worrying about lately will start to seem trivial now. People around you are jovial. You may receive some kind of proposal. For those of you who are single, it can mean marriage. If already attached, it can be a suggestion of a romantic weekend away.

Wednesday the 24th. Home and family life should be buzzing with activity. Do not expect a boring Hanukkah or Christmas Eve. For Leos stuck at work, it will be an excellent time for tying up loose ends. A major task can be completed. Anything else must wait, even if people are impatient.

Thursday the 25th. Merry Christmas! Spending the holiday with your family will be delightful for the most part. You may find yourself frustrated with your partner for overindulging. Console yourself with the fact that this day occurs only once a year.

Friday the 26th. The friction that you may have experienced between you and your partner yesterday should be gone now. You are likely to have a romantic day together. Children may need you as a play companion, and this can be lots of fun for you.

Saturday the 27th. This will be the perfect time for going away on a romantic weekend trip. Any kind of change of scene will be good, but traveling with a partner will be even better. If you have children, they probably will appreciate a break as well.

Sunday the 28th. There should be a lot of closeness between you and a lover. If you are single, go along to a party. The opportunity to meet somebody very well matched to you arises. And you will have a good time seeing people you know.

Monday the 29th. Work matters are likely to be at the forefront of your mind. You may be worrying if you are stranded out of town, perhaps because of the weather. Do not panic. It is very likely that your story will be viewed as genuine.

Tuesday the 30th. Work may be chaotic through neglect or because everyone is out of sync after the holiday break. It may take a while to figure out your priorities. If you are not at work, stop worrying about what may be going on in your absence.

Wednesday the 31st. There will be some very interesting developments in one-on-one relationships. If you are single, that situation can turn around, especially if you go to a New Year's Eve party. There is deep rapport between long-established couples.